Legislating for
Sustainable Fisheries

Law, Justice, and Development

The Law, Justice, and Development papers are intended to provide insights into aspects of law and justice that are relevant to the development process. New legal and judicial reform activities related to the World Bank's work will be presented, as well as analyses of domestic and international law. The series is intended to be accessible to a broad audience as well as to legal practitioners.

Series editor: Rudolf V. Van Puymbroeck

Legislating for Sustainable Fisheries

A Guide to Implementing the 1993 FAO Compliance
Agreement and 1995 UN Fish Stocks Agreement

William Edeson
Senior Legal Officer
Legal Office
Food and Agriculture Organization of the United Nations

David Freestone
Chief Counsel
Environmentally and Socially Sustainable Development
and International Law Group
The World Bank

Elly Gudmundsdottir
Counsel
Europe and Central Asia Group
The World Bank

The World Bank
Washington, D.C.

Library of Congress Cataloging-in-Publication Data

Edeson, W. R. (William R.)
  Legislating for sustainable fisheries : a guide to implementing the
1993 FAO Compliance Agreement and 1995 UN Fish Stocks Agreement /
William Edeson, David Freestone, Elly Gudmundsdottir.
    p. cm. — (Law, justice, and development)
Includes bibliographical references and index.
  ISBN 0-8213-4993-7
  1. Fishery law and legislation. 2. Fishery conservation. I.
Freestone, David. II. Gudmundsdottir, Elly, 1964– III. Title. IV.
Series.
  K3895 .E34 2001
  343.73'07692—dc21

                                                    2001045660

POD by LSI

Contents

Abstract

Increasing concerns have been raised about the sustainability of many fish stocks. A number of international instruments, both voluntary and binding, have been formulated to address this. Two important binding agreements that are designed to address this problem on a global basis are the 1993 FAO Compliance Agreement and the 1995 UN Fish Stocks Agreement. However, neither of these agreements has yet entered into force. For some countries, particularly smaller developing countries, the very complexity of the task of transposing the provisions of these agreements into national law may itself be an obstacle to, or cause of delay in, becoming a party to them. The purpose of this guide is to facilitate the ratification or acceptance of these agreements in such countries. The guide provides an outline of some of the most significant provisions of the two agreements and a "tool kit" of the various approaches that have already been used by those few states that have already enacted national legislation to meet the obligations and the objectives contained in these two agreements.

Preface

This work is intended as a practical guide for the parliamentary drafter or legislator faced with the task of transposing the obligations of two significant fisheries agreements into national law: the 1993 Agreement to Promote Compliance with International Conservation and Management Measures by Fishing Vessels on the High Seas, and the 1995 Agreement for the Implementation of the Provisions of the United Nations Convention on the Law of the Sea of 10 December 1982 Relating to the Conservation and Management of Straddling Fish Stocks and Highly Migratory Fish Stocks. These two agreements will be referred to as the "Compliance Agreement" and the "Fish Stocks Agreement," respectively. Both agreements derive their significance from the 1982 UN Law of the Sea Convention, but each, in different but equally novel ways, develops the 1982 regime.

Although both agreements have attracted a great deal of attention, at the time of this writing the number of parties to each remains relatively small and neither agreement has yet entered into force. There are obviously a large number of reasons for this, but informal discussions suggest that for some states, particularly smaller ones, the task of transposing the complex provisions of these agreements into their national law is itself an obstacle to, or a delaying factor in, ratification or acceptance. It is hoped that this Guide will be of some assistance in that regard.

The development of this Guide posed a number of challenges for us. It is not intended as a comprehensive assessment of all the implementing legislation passed to date; indeed it does not address all the minutiae of implementation. Rather it seeks to provide an understanding of the issues that need to be addressed when transforming the obligations of the aforementioned international instruments into national law, and to provide examples of the sorts of drafting techniques that other countries have used to achieve this goal. It certainly does not propose a model law—a device that, given the interrelation of the agreements with existing national legal frameworks, we did not regard as appropriate. However, the number of states that have enacted relevant legislation is relatively small. Most have used amending legislation, rather than freestanding acts. Amending legislation is notoriously difficult to understand unless one has a good familiarity with the parent legislation; therefore we have found it to be of limited use for this Guide. As a result of our pragmatic choices, we present, wherever possible, a range of implementation possibilities rather than one approach. These choices certainly do not represent the endorsement of one state's legislation over another. Our hope is that this Guide will help increase the number of states able to accept these two important fisheries law instruments, that there will soon be a much greater number of new examples of national implementing laws available, and that the need for this Guide will soon be rendered otiose.

Washington, D.C., and Rome

Acknowledgments

The authors would like to acknowledge the help and support of a number of entities and individuals during the preparation of the Guide. First and foremost, we would like to thank the Government of Iceland for its support of this project, through the World Bank Icelandic Consultant Trust Fund. We would also like to thank the World Bank Legal Vice Presidency and the FAO Legal Office for providing the financial support to publish this Guide.

Several friends and colleagues reviewed various drafts. We would particularly like to acknowledge David Balton, Director of Marine Conservation at the U.S. State Department; Larry Christy, Chief of Development Law Service at the Legal Office of FAO; and Annick Van Houtte and Blaise Kuemlangan, legal officers at the Development Law Service. Last but not least, our thanks to Rudolf V. Van Puymbroeck who oversaw the arduous task of transposing an unruly final draft into what we hope is now a presentable text.

Acronyms and Abbreviations

AFMA	Australian Fisheries Management Authority
AFZ	Australian Fishing Zone
CCAMLR	Convention on the Conservation of Antarctic Marine Living Resources
COFI	Committee on Fisheries (FAO)
CWP	Coordinating Working Party
DWFS	Distant Water Fishing States
EEZ	Exclusive Economic Zone
FAO	Food and Agriculture Organization of the United Nations
FSA	Fish Stocks Agreement
HSREG	High Seas Vessel Registration Database System
IPOA	International Plan of Action
IUU (Fishing)	Illegal, Unreported and Unregulated (Fishing)
OECS	Organization of Eastern Caribbean States
RFB	Regional Fisheries Body
RFO	Regional Fisheries Organization
UNCED	United Nations Conference on Environment and Development
WTO	World Trade Organization

INTRODUCTION

The issue of straddling fish stocks and highly migratory fish stocks was taken up during the preparatory meetings leading to the 1992 United Nations Conference on Environment and Development (UNCED). During UNCED, participants expressed serious concerns about the state of world fisheries, in particular the mismanagement of straddling and highly migratory fish stocks in the high seas. UNCED adopted Agenda 21, which in chapter 17 called, inter alia, for an intergovernmental conference under the auspices of the United Nations to promote effective implementation of the provisions of the 1982 UN Convention on the Law of the Sea.[1] The conference was to identify and assess existing problems related to the conservation and management of such stocks, to consider means of improving cooperation on fisheries among states, and to formulate appropriate recommendations.

UNCED also called on states to take effective action to deter re-flagging of fishing boats.[2] In the run-up to UNCED, the Mexican government had sponsored an International Conference on Responsible Fishing, held in Cancun, Mexico in May 1992. Representatives from 49 states, holding 70 percent of the world's fishing capacity, attended the conference, which adopted by consensus the 1992 Cancun Declaration on Responsible Fishing. The Cancun Declaration called on the United Nations Food and Agriculture Organization (FAO) to begin work on the development of an international code of conduct for responsible fishing.

Against this background, the international community moved into what can be described as a two-track approach to the problems of high seas overfishing. One component was the negotiation of an international agreement to deal specifically with straddling fish stocks and highly migratory fish stocks; the other was the development of a code of conduct, which was intended to be voluntary in nature and cover much more than high seas fishing.[3] At the same time, FAO was working on a compliance agreement, which was intended to be an integral part of the voluntary code of conduct and to reduce fishing on the high seas in ways—such as, notably, re-flagging of

1

ships—that ran counter to internationally agreed conservation and management measures.

Following the 1992 UNCED recommendation, the United Nations Conference on Straddling Fish Stocks and Highly Migratory Fish Stocks convened the first of its six sessions in April 1993. At its sixth session, from July 24 to August 8, 1995, the conference concluded its work with the adoption of a legally binding instrument—the Fish Stocks Agreement. Meanwhile, as the Cancun meeting had proposed, a work plan had been developed for the elaboration of a code of conduct on responsible fishing under the auspices of FAO. FAO also took responsibility for developing a legal agreement to address the issue of re-flagging of fishing boats as called for in Agenda 21. In November 1993, the FAO Conference adopted the Compliance Agreement. Negotiations on the Code of Conduct for Responsible Fishing (or Fisheries as it was renamed) also began in 1993, but the final text was not adopted until November 1995, after the final text of the Fish Stocks Agreement had been agreed upon.

Both the Compliance Agreement and the Fish Stocks Agreement are framed in accordance with the 1982 UN Convention and seek to develop and strengthen its provisions.

The purpose of the Compliance Agreement—which was initially conceived as an instrument to close a legal loophole in regional and species fisheries arrangements whereby fishing vessels could change their state of registration ("re-flag") in order to evade or avoid the obligations of an international arrangement—is to reinforce the effectiveness of international fisheries conservation and management measures. It does this by redefining and reinforcing in a number of specific ways the concept of flag state responsibility for the activities of fishing vessels flying the flag of a state that is party to the agreement. It also seeks to provide means to ensure the free flow of information on all high seas fishing operations.[4]

The objective of the Fish Stocks Agreement is "to ensure the long-term conservation and sustainable use of straddling fish stocks and highly migratory fish stocks through effective implementation of the relevant provisions of the [Law of the Sea] Convention."[5] To this end, the agreement focuses on creating a detailed framework for the management of these fish stocks. The agreement addresses the conservation and management of straddling and highly migratory fish stocks, as well as the conservation of marine ecosystems as a whole.

Both agreements are international law instruments addressing the nature of states' obligations to one another at the international level. Both agreements also seek to define with a high degree of specificity the ways in which state parties should meet these obligations—which is unusual in global fisheries agreements. For this reason, if for no other, implementing legislation will be necessary in most countries to meet these requirements as a precondition to state ratification or acceptance. In most countries this will usually call for new legislation, but, depending on the legislation already in place, some countries may be able to implement the agreements through changes to current legislation, new regulations, or other subsidiary legislation.

As noted in the preface, the purpose of this Guide is to identify some of the more difficult issues that are likely to arise in the process of transposition of these two international instruments into national law. At the time of writing, most of the existing legislation designed to effect this transposition has been in developed countries. However, the Guide attempts to extract the key issues that will need to be addressed by any national administration—be it in a developed or developing country.

In creating this Guide we have made extensive use of the national legislation that has already been developed and, in a number of countries, passed. At the time of writing, national legislation from the following countries was available: Canada, Norway, Iceland, the Republic of South Africa, the United States, Australia, and New Zealand.

In addition to these countries, Namibia has on 1 August 2001 brought into force the Marine Resources Act. This act implements both the Compliance Agreement and the Fish Stocks Agreement into national law. Furthermore, in 1997 the Organization of Eastern Caribbean States (OECS), in collaboration with FAO, held a workshop on the issue of implementation of the Compliance Agreement and the Fish Stocks Agreement in the Eastern Caribbean; draft legislation (hereafter "OECS draft") adopted by that workshop has also been used in developing this Guide. The OECS draft itself is in part based on the earlier "Guidelines for the Implementation in National Legislation of the Agreement to Promote Compliance with International Conservation and Management Measures by Fishing Vessels on the High Seas," published by the FAO Legal Office in August 1994.

PART ONE

Implementing the Compliance Agreement

The purpose of this section is to identify the key issues in the Compliance Agreement[6] that need to be transposed into national legislation and suggest how this might be done, drawing where appropriate on the legislation of states that have already undertaken this task.

As indicated above, in most countries, following the agreement will require new national laws. Depending on the legislation already in place, however, some countries may be able to implement the agreement through changes to current legislation, new regulations, or other subsidiary legislation. Any reference to "national legislation" in this section may mean any of these legal devices.

The most important provisions of the Compliance Agreement, from the point of view of a state implementing legislation, are those related to the responsibility of the flag state and to the gathering and exchange of information. An essential starting point for the parties to the agreement would be deciding which authority should be responsible for carrying out the duties according to the agreement and defining what those duties are.

Administration

It is important for a state that is party to the agreement to make an initial decision as to which national bodies will have the responsibility to carry out the actions or functions that are required to be performed by the party's government under the agreement.[7] That authority would be responsible for carrying out the following duties of the agreement:

- High seas fishing authorizations: the authorization, denial, revocation, or suspension of high seas fishing authorizations;
- Setting up and maintaining a record of high seas fishing vessels;
- Collection and sharing of information; and
- Enforcement.

5

The authority that would carry out this responsibility would have to be designated by national legislation. The duties could be spelled out in a separate regulation. A model for such a provision is set out in FAO's "Guidelines for the Implementation in National Legislation of the Agreement to Promote Compliance with International Conservation and Management Measures by Fishing Vessels on the High Seas."[8] It reads as follows:

3. (1) This Act shall be administered by the [Chief Fisheries Officer] [Director of Fisheries] appointed pursuant to [relevant fisheries law] who shall be responsible for:

    (a) maintaining a record of all fishing vessels in respect of which high seas fishing licenses have been issued under this Act, . . . ;

    (b) collection of statistics concerning fish stocks and fishing on the high seas;

    (c) the monitoring, control and surveillance of the operations of fishing vessels of [Enacting State] on the high seas;

    (d) the issue, variation, suspension and revocation of licenses for fishing on the high seas;

    (e) the collection of fees in respect of licenses of fishing vessels;

    (f) the giving of such information and the making of such reports to FAO and other parties to the Agreement as is required of [Enacting State] pursuant to Articles V and VI of the Agreement;

    (g) the taking of appropriate measures in cooperation with other States for the implementation of Articles VII and VIII of the Agreement;

    (h) . . .

    (i) the taking of all such other measures as the [Chief Fisheries Officer] [Director of Fisheries] may consider appropriate for the implementation of the Agreement and this Act.

. . .

(5) This Act shall be enforced by authorized officers acting subject to the directions of the [Chief Fisheries Officer] [Director of Fisheries]. . . .

This is an important provision because it lays out how the important elements of the Compliance Agreement will need to be put into effect.

Flag State Responsibility

The concept of flag state responsibility in respect of fishing vessels operating on the high seas is spelled out in Article III of the Compliance Agreement, which is the first global agreement to address this issue.[9] It requires parties to take such measures as may be necessary to ensure that fishing vessels entitled to fly their flag do not engage in any activity that undermines the effectiveness of any international conservation and management measures.

"International conservation and management measures" are defined in Article I(b) of the Compliance Agreement as "measures to conserve or manage one or more species of living marine resources that are adopted and applied in accordance with the relevant rules of international law as reflected in the 1982 United Nations Convention on the Law of the Sea. Such measures may be adopted by global, regional or sub-regional fisheries organizations, subject to the rights and obligations of their members, or by treaties or other international agreements."

It will probably not be possible for these provisions to be spelled out definitively in national law because the definition looks ahead to future conservation and management measures, as well as backward at existing measures. To do so would involve making it an offense in national law for a fishing vessel in the state in question to engage in any activity that undermines such conservation and management measures. In some jurisdictions the need for prosecutors to state with precision the charge that the defendant must answer may cause problems with such a wide definition. One device that may be employed to introduce greater certainty is to delegate to the minister the power and responsibility to list those measures to which the act applies. This does, however, require a continuing commitment to update this list on a regular basis.

Fishing Authorization

According to the agreement, parties shall not allow any of their flag vessels to fish on the high seas unless they have been authorized to do so by the appropriate national authorities.[10] Authorized fishing vessels must fish in accordance with conditions of the authorization.

Here, national legislative provisions have to set up the necessary framework to authorize high seas fishing. It will also be necessary for parties to describe the application process—where and how to apply, what the cost will be, and so on.

The U.S. High Seas Fishing Compliance Act of 1995 deals with the matter in the following way:

(1) The owner or operator of a high seas fishing vessel may apply for a permit under this section by completing an application form prescribed by the Secretary.

(2) The application form shall contain—

    (A) the vessel's name, previous names (if known), official numbers, and port of record;

    (B) the vessel's previous flags (if any);

    (C) the vessel's International Radio Call Sign (if any);

    (D) the names and addresses of the vessel's owners and operators;

    (E) where and when the vessel was built;

    (F) the type of vessel;

    (G) the vessel's length; and

    (H) any other information the Secretary requires for the purposes of implementing the Agreement.[11]

The law will have to be clear about the conditions that may be imposed on the granting of the authorizations. Many countries will probably find it convenient to give the authority responsible for the implementation of the act the power to address this issue in part through regulation.

In addition to these conditions, certain other obligations are imposed directly on the state. First, according to Article III.3 of the Compliance Agreement:

No Party shall authorize any fishing vessel entitled to fly its flag to be used for fishing on the high seas unless the Party is satisfied that it is able, taking into account the links that exist between it and the fishing vessel concerned, to exercise effectively its responsibilities under this Agreement in respect of that fishing vessel.

A key concept here is the "link" between the vessel and the flag state. The agreement puts this in terms of the ability of that state "to exercise effectively its responsibilities under this Agreement" in respect of its vessels. Parties first have to decide for themselves what kind of link vessels need to have to the flag state in order to meet the requirements of this paragraph and then express that in legislation. Parties may wish to spell out in detail the factors that should be taken into consideration in determining whether the government will be able to exercise effectively its responsibilities under the agreement with regard to a particular vessel. Alternatively, the determination could be left to the discretion of the authority responsible for the implementation of the act.[12]

The U.S. High Seas Fishing Compliance Act of 1995 leaves it to the secretary of commerce to decide when the link is sufficient:

> The Secretary may not issue a permit to a vessel unless the Secretary is satisfied that the United States will be able to exercise effectively its responsibilities under the Agreement with respect to that vessel.[13]

In contrast, the Marine Living Resources Act of the Republic of South Africa gives the minister the power to "issue a high seas fishing license in respect of a local fishing vessel, subject to the conditions that he or she considers appropriate."[14]

In general, it would be in the best interests of the parties to have strong links to vessels registered in their state. If a vessel has no substantial economic or physical links with the flag state other than the fact of registration, then it could become costly and difficult to monitor the activities of such a vessel to ensure that it does not undermine the effectiveness of international conservation and management measures. Under such circumstances, where the vessel is not landing its catch in the flag state or otherwise contributing to the flag state's economy, except through registration fees, the costs of such measures would almost certainly outweigh any benefits from registering the vessel.[15] Indeed, the flag state may wish to require that the vessel in question have a certain percentage of local ownership, that it return to the ports of the registering state periodically, or impose other requirements that would enable the flag state to exercise control over the vessel in question.[16]

In situations in which a vessel has changed its flag state, parties to the Compliance Agreement are obliged not to grant fishing authorizations to any such vessel if that vessel is still serving a period of suspension of its authorization in the former flag state, or during a period of three years following the withdrawal of high seas fishing authorization by the former flag state.[17] In this way, the Compliance Agreement seeks to limit the freedom of vessels that have a bad compliance record in high seas fisheries to "shop around" for new flags.

There are, however, some exceptions and limitations to this obligation, particularly in cases in which it can be shown that there has been a bona fide change in vessel ownership, or in which the new flag state—taking into account, among other things, the circumstances in which the authorization was withdrawn—makes a determination that to grant the authorization would not undermine the objects and purposes of the agreement.

The U.S. 1995 High Seas Fishing Compliance Act puts this mandatory condition forward in the following way (in section 104):

(b) Eligibility—

  (1) Any vessel of the United States is eligible to receive a permit under this section, unless the vessel was previously authorized to be used for fishing on the high seas by a foreign nation, and

   (A) the foreign nation suspended such authorization because the vessel undermined the effectiveness of international conservation and management measures, and the suspension has not expired; or

   (B) the foreign nation, within the last three years preceding application for a permit under this section, withdrew such authorization because the vessel undermined the effectiveness of international conservation and management measures.

  (2) The restriction in paragraph (1) does not apply if ownership of the vessel has changed since the vessel undermined the effectiveness of international conservation and management measures, and the new owner has provided sufficient evidence to the Secretary demonstrating that the previous owner or operator has no further legal, beneficial or financial interest in, or control of, the vessel.

  (3) The restriction in paragraph (1) does not apply if the Secretary makes a determination that issuing a permit would not subvert the purposes of the Agreement.

Other Obligations

The agreement further requires the following:

Marking of vessels. The flag state is to ensure that its vessels are properly marked.[18] This could be put forward in national legislation as one of the conditions for receiving a fishing authorization. This is proposed in the OECS draft and implemented in the U.S. High Seas Fishing Compliance Act of 1995, section 103(d)(1).

For an appropriate example of the marking of vessels, the Compliance Agreement refers to the FAO Standard Specifications for the Marking and Identification of Fishing Vessels, which is also cited by both the OECS draft and the U.S. legislation (these FAO specifications are reproduced in Appendix III).

Information on the fishing operation. The vessels of a flag state are to provide the party with the necessary information on their operation, including fishing area, catch, and landing data, as may be necessary to enable the state to fulfill its obligations under the agreement.[19] This could also be put forward as a condition of receiving fishing authorization.

Enforcement measures. Parties are required to take enforcement measures against any of their flag vessels that act in contravention of the agreement provisions. Sanctions must be of sufficient gravity to be effective in securing compliance and to deprive offenders of the benefits accruing from their illegal activities and are to include, for serious offenses, refusal, suspension, or withdrawal of the authorization to fish on the high seas.[20] This will usually involve legislation proscribing such acts as criminal.

Each party has to decide what authority is to carry out the enforcement procedures necessary for the agreement and what the powers and duties of that authority are to be.

The Marine Living Resources Act of the Republic of South Africa[21] and the U.S. High Seas Fishing Compliance Act of 1995[22] both delegate the power to decide who is to be the enforcement authority to the appropriate minister (secretary) but both contain detailed provisions with respect to the power of the enforcement authority.

Section 107(c) on the "Powers of Enforcement Officers," of the U.S. act reads as follows:

(1) Any officer who is authorized under subsection (a) to enforce the provisions of this title may—

    (A) with or without a warrant or other process—

        (i) arrest any person, if the officer has reasonable cause to believe that such person has committed an act prohibited by paragraph (6), (7), (8), or (9) of section 106;

(ii)   board, and search or inspect, any high seas fishing vessel;

(iii)   seize any high seas fishing vessel (together with its fishing gear, furniture, appurtenances, stores and cargo) used or employed in, or with respect to which it reasonably appears that such vessel was used or employed in, the violation of any provision of this title or any regulation or permit issued under this title;

(iv)   seize any living marine resource (wherever found) taken or retained, in any manner, in connection with or as a result of the commission of any act prohibited by section 106;

(v)   seize any other evidence related to any violation of any provision of this title or any regulation or permit issued under this title;

(B)   execute any warrant or other process issued by any court of competent jurisdiction; and

(C)   exercise any other lawful authority. . . .

The OECS draft includes a similar provision.

> Enforcement measures and sanctions have to be implemented through national legislation. The legislation has to define what is an offence and what penalties or sanctions apply when that offence takes place. Each party may determine for itself the sanctions that it regards adequately severe, as long as they fulfill the requirements of the agreement.

Record of fishing vessels. The flag state is to maintain a record of fishing vessels entitled to fly its flag and authorized to fish on the high seas and take such measures as may be necessary to ensure that all such fishing vessels are entered in that record.[23] It would be preferable to require the establishment and maintenance of such a record by national law.

Use of the term "record," instead of the more common term "register," underlines the fact that it is the system of granting fishing authorization that is to be the primary means of control rather than the vessel register itself.[24] However, some countries, such as the Republic of South Africa, still use the term "register" for their record, without seeming to aim at a system of registration different than that described in the Compliance Agreement.[25]

Although Article IV does not specify what is to be the substance of this record, some mandatory provisions can be read from Article VI on "Exchange of Information." It is through this article that the full impact of the scheme established by the Compliance Agreement emerges.

Exchange of Information

The second main pillar of the Compliance Agreement, apart from the flag state responsibility, is found in Article VI, which deals with the exchange of information. It is designed to ensure an adequate flow of information on high seas fisheries.

Each party to the agreement is to make certain that information regarding high seas fisheries outlined in Article VI is available to FAO, which will pass this information on to all contracting parties, and, upon request, to global, regional, and subregional fisheries management organizations.

Each party shall make available to FAO information on each fishing vessel entered into the record that each party is required to maintain under Article IV[26] and, to the extent practicable, certain additional information from the same record.[27] Each party shall also notify FAO promptly of any modifications to this information[28] and of additions and deletions, including the reasons for deletion, of a vessel from the record.[29] In turn, FAO shall circulate this information periodically. Information regarding additions to, or deletions from, the record shall be circulated promptly[30] to all parties and also, upon request,[31] individually to any global, regional, or subregional fisheries organizations.[32]

Each party is also required to provide FAO promptly with all information regarding activities of fishing vessels flying its flag that undermine the effectiveness of international conservation and management measures, including the identity of the vessel and of any measures imposed.[33] Each party, if it has reasonable grounds to believe that a fishing vessel not entitled to fly its flag has engaged in any activity that undermines the effectiveness of such conservation and management measures, is to draw this to the attention of the flag state concerned and, as appropriate, may provide FAO with a summary of such evidence.[34] Each party is also required to inform FAO of any authorization in respect of a vessel previously registered in the territory of another party where a period of suspension has not expired, or where an authorization to fish has been withdrawn.[35] Reports on measures imposed by a party may be subject to such limitations as may be required by national legislation with respect to confidentiality.[36]

In support of the Compliance Agreement, a High Seas Vessel Registration Database System (HSREG) has been created at FAO to facilitate the monitoring of vessels licensed to fish on the high seas.[37] The database currently contains information on licensed vessels from Canada, Japan, and the United States, but will hopefully increase considerably in the future. Flag states can in any event provide such information quite apart from the agreement, subject only to confidentiality requirements and other restraints that might be imposed by national law. The national law may have to be changed in some countries to permit such information to be supplied to an international agency.

The duties of the flag states to provide FAO with the detailed information according to Article VI will need to be specified in legislation. Some countries may have a fishing vessels register already in place that may serve as a base for the high seas fishing vessels record. Most existing national registers cover all vessels indiscriminately and changes may have to be made in their system to develop a separate national register for fishing vessels.

The information to be provided according to Article VI already should be available from the record required under Article IV of the Compliance Agreement, from the operation of the authorization scheme in Article III, and from the international cooperation provisions in Article V. The obligations under Article VI should therefore not create too heavy a burden for the administration.[38]

The U.S. High Seas Fishing Compliance Act contains detailed provisions with respect to Article VI and is quoted here in full:

Sec. 105. *Responsibilities of the Secretary.*

(a) Record—The Secretary shall maintain an automated file or record of high seas fishing vessels issued permits under section 104, including all information submitted under section 104(c)(2).

(b) Information to FAO—The Secretary, in cooperation with the Secretary of State and the Secretary of the department in which the Coast Guard is operating shall—

　　(1) make available to FAO information contained in the record maintained under subsection (a);

(2)   promptly notify FAO of changes in such information;

(3)   promptly notify FAO of additions to or deletions from the record, and the reason for any deletion;

(4)   convey to FAO information relating to any permit granted under section 104(b)(3), including the vessel's identity, owner or operator, and factors relevant to the Secretary's determination to issue the permit;

(5)   report promptly to FAO all relevant information regarding any activities of high seas fishing vessels that undermine the effectiveness of international conservation and management measures, including the identity of the vessels and any sanctions imposed; and

(6)   provide the FAO a summary of evidence regarding any activities of foreign vessels that undermine the effectiveness of international conservation and management measures.

(c)   Information to flag nations—If the Secretary, in cooperation with the Secretary of State and the Secretary of the department in which the Coast Guard is operating, has reasonable grounds to believe that a foreign vessel has engaged in activities undermining the effectiveness of international conservation and management measures, the Secretary shall—

(1)   provide to the flag nation information, including appropriate evidentiary material, relating to those activities; and

(2)   when such foreign vessel is voluntarily in a United States port, promptly notify the flag nation and, if requested by the flag nation, make arrangements to undertake such lawful investigatory measures as may be considered necessary to establish whether the vessel has been used contrary to the provisions of the Agreement.

The Scope of Application of the Compliance Agreement

According to Article II.1, the Compliance Agreement is to apply to "all fishing vessels that are used or intended for fishing on the high seas." This broad application is limited, however, in two ways in the agreement itself—first, through the definition of fishing vessels, and second, by allowing the parties to exempt certain vessels from the detailed administrative provisions of the agreement.

Definition of Fishing Vessels

The definition of fishing vessels in Article I(a) covers "any vessel used or intended for use for the purposes of the commercial exploitation of living marine resources, including mother ships and any other vessels directly engaged in such fishing operations." This definition was intended to be restrictive, as it excludes any support vessels not directly engaged in fishing operations, and it was a point of contention in the negotiations.[39]

Exemption of Vessels under 24 Meters

The second limitation concerns the right of parties to the agreement to exempt vessels of less than 24 meters in length from the application of some of the detailed administrative provisions of the agreement.[40]

It is important to note that this exemption does not apply to the Compliance Agreement's main obligation—ensuring that the vessels concerned do not undermine the effectiveness of international conservation and management measures. This is confirmed in Article II: "A party may exempt fishing vessels of less than 24 metres in length entitled to fly its flag from the application of this Agreement *unless the Party determines that such an exemption would undermine the object and purpose of this Agreement. . .*" This is strengthened further by the provision in Article III stating that in the event that a party has granted an exemption for fishing vessels of less than 24 meters "such Party shall nevertheless take effective measures in respect of any such fishing vessel that undermines the effectiveness of international conservation and management measures. These measures shall be such as to ensure that the fishing vessel ceases to engage in activities that undermine the effectiveness of the international conservation and management measures."

Parties to the agreement should also keep in mind that the Fish Stocks Agreement does not contain an exemption like this. So, if a state that is party to both agreements were to decide to exempt its vessels under 24 meters from the Compliance Agreement, those vessels would not be exempted from the Fish Stocks Agreement while fishing for straddling fish stocks and highly migratory fish stocks on the high seas.

In fishing regions where bordering coastal states have not yet declared exclusive economic zones (EEZs) or equivalent zones of national jurisdiction over fisheries, the coastal states that are parties to the agreement may agree upon minimum length limits collectively for their own flag vessels operating exclusively in those regions. Vessels below those lengths would then be automatically exempted in recognition of the need to exclude purely inshore fisheries.[41]

Canadian and Norwegian Practice

Two countries, Canada and Norway, have given effect to the Compliance Agreement by means of short regulations that assume sufficient powers already exist under existing laws to give effect to it in most respects.

The Compliance Agreement has been implemented into Canadian national law by means of a short regulation enacted pursuant to the Canadian Coastal Fisheries Protection Act, part XIII. The regulation enables the minister to issue to a vessel that is subject to Canada's jurisdiction a license that authorizes the use of the vessel in fishing or transshipping fish in "waters other than Canadian waters" if it would not contravene or undermine any international fisheries conservation scheme, or in the case of fishing or transshipping of fish in waters subject to the jurisdiction of another state, that the activity is authorized by a competent authority of that state.[42]

The regulation prohibits fishing or transshipping of fish by a vessel "subject to the jurisdiction of Canada" except under the authority of a license issued under the regulations, though an exception is made in respect of fishing taking place for licenses issued under the Atlantic Fishery Regulations (1985) and under the Pacific Fishery Regulations (1993).[43]

The regulation does not deal with the provision of information required under the FAO Compliance Agreement—on the basis, it would seem, that there is already sufficient legal authority to provide the necessary information.

Norway, which has accepted the Compliance Agreement, has, like Canada, given effect to the agreement by means of a regulation that draws upon existing legal powers in areas beyond national jurisdiction. In particular, with regard to the provision of information that is essential to the achievement of the objectives of the Compliance Agreement, the Register of Norwegian Fishing Vessels has existed since 1917. This register is considered to be a sufficient basis for the new register required in respect of Norwegian vessels authorized to fish on the high seas.[44] The regulation prepared for this purpose contains the elements discussed below.[45]

It applies to fishing vessels flying the Norwegian flag and fishing for stocks not regulated by Norwegian authorities. Such a vessel is prohibited from fishing unless the vessel has first registered with the Directorate of Fisheries. Each vessel registration is valid for one year. However, the directorate may deny registration in the following situations:

a)   the fishery is considered to be in conflict with Norwegian fisheries interests,

b)   international agreements make this necessary,

c)   the fishery is regulated by regional or subregional fisheries management organisations or arrangements,

d)   it is necessary for conducting or completing fishing or hunting activities in a rational or proper manner.[46]

The directorate also has the power to delete from the registration list any vessel that has violated any regulation in force in the area concerned.

There are also reporting obligations, namely when a fishing activity is started and concluded, as well as weekly catch reports with respect to specified species and areas.

In effect, the Norwegian approach has been to utilize existing legal powers to enact these regulations. It focuses on the powers of the flag state over its vessels. However, the requirement of registration will enable Norway to fulfill its other major obligation under the Compliance Agreement, namely to inform FAO of the details of its vessels fishing on the high seas, as required by Article VI of the Compliance Agreement. Although the regulations outlined above appear at first sight minimalist in their character, they in fact are based on a substantial pre-existing legal regime available to Norway to control its vessels on the high seas. Further, they should be seen in conjunction with another regulation introduced by Norway which is aimed at combating illegal or unregulated fishing by vessels flying the flag of other states, which is discussed below.

In addition, Norway has introduced a further regulation stating that an application for a license may be denied if the vessel or the vessel owner has taken part in an unregulated fishery in international waters on a fish stock subject to regulations in waters under Norwegian fisheries jurisdiction. The purpose of this provision is to provide the opportunity to blacklist and ban a vessel from fishing in Norwegian waters even if it was operated by others when it participated in the unregulated high seas fishery.

The Compliance Agreement: A Summary

The agreement requires the following issues to be implemented into the national legislation of its parties:

- A definition of the duties of the flag state, according to the agreement, and designation of the national authority responsible for carrying them out.

- Provisions making it unlawful for flag vessels to undermine the effectiveness of international conservation and management measures, and providing a mechanism for authorities to ensure that the law is respected.

- Mandatory fishing authorizations for flag vessels fishing on the high seas.

- Mandatory conditions for flag vessels receiving a fishing authorization.

- Proper marking of fishing vessels.

- Information on fishing operations.

- Enforcement measures and sanctions.

- Establishment and maintenance of record of flag vessels fishing on the high seas.

- The duties of the flag state to provide FAO with information.

PART TWO

Implementing the Fish Stocks Agreement

Parts I and II

Article 2 of the Fish Stocks Agreement sets out its overarching objective: "to ensure the long-term conservation and sustainable use of straddling fish stocks and highly migratory fish stocks through effective implementation of the relevant provisions of the [Law of the Sea] Convention." To this end, the agreement focuses on creating a detailed framework for the management of these fish stocks. It can be seen from the preamble of the agreement, however, that it does not only address issues concerned with the fish stocks themselves and their capture, but also places their conservation and management squarely within the wider context of the need to avoid adverse impacts on the marine environment, of the preservation of marine biodiversity, and of the integrity of the marine ecosystem.

The Fish Stocks Agreement will enter into force 30 days after the date of deposit of the thirtieth instrument of ratification or accession. At the time of writing, 57 states have signed the agreement, and 27 have ratified it.[47]

The Fish Stocks Agreement applies, "unless otherwise provided," to the conservation and management of straddling fish stocks and highly migratory fish stocks "beyond areas under national jurisdiction."[48] However, Article 6, concerning the precautionary approach, and Article 7, concerning compatibility of conservation measures established for the high seas and those adopted for areas under national jurisdiction, also apply within areas under national jurisdiction. Likewise, the coastal state is required to apply—mutatis mutandis—the general principles set out in Article 5 in the exercise of its sovereign rights concerning straddling fish stocks and highly migratory fish stocks.

With regard to national implementation of the Fish Stocks Agreement, the main provisions that call for implementation through national legislation are Articles 5, 6, and 7, which expressly apply within the EEZ. There are, however,

The Main Elements of the Fish Stocks Agreement

1. The agreement requires coastal states and distant water fishing states (DWFS) to ensure that the conservation and management measures, which are created within the EEZ and on the high seas, are compatible.

2. The agreement sets out general principles for the conservation and management of straddling fish stocks and highly migratory fish stocks, including the precautionary approach, which parties to the agreement are to apply on the high seas as well as within their EEZ.

3. The agreement specifies the duties of the flag states with respect to their vessels fishing on the high seas for straddling fish stocks and highly migratory fish stocks.

4. The agreement contains detailed rules on the establishment and operation of subregional or regional fisheries management organizations or arrangements (RFOs) which are to establish conservation and management measures on the high seas. Parties to the agreement are obliged to join RFOs or agree to comply with the measures they create. Otherwise they will not be allowed to fish in the areas where these management and conservation measures apply.

5. The agreement introduces innovative provisions on enforcement for non-flag states, and a new concept of port-state jurisdiction in respect of fishing vessels.

6. The agreement contains detailed provisions on peaceful dispute settlement.

a number of other issues to be addressed at the national level—notably the implementation of those provisions of the agreement that require state parties to impose duties and obligations directly on natural or legal persons.

This section seeks to identify the issues contained in the Fish Stocks Agreement that require specific implementation at the national level. Drawing heavily on the practice of those states that have already passed national legislation, it also seeks to suggest ways in which the issues may be transposed into national law.

The Fish Stocks Agreement envisages the implementation of its norms at both the international and the national levels. Many of the norms it contains require development, adoption, and implementation within the context of an appropriate subregional or regional management organization, with competence to establish conservation and management measures for highly migratory fish stocks. The obligations of the individual state party under the agreement are therefore to ensure that its own legal system is able to provide the necessary legal means and modalities to accommodate the new concepts, the expanded jurisdictional powers, and other general requirements of the agreement, but also able to utilize these specifically in the context of the appropriate regional or subregional management organization. Although implementation at the international level is beyond the scope of this Guide, it will be necessary to refer to aspects of international implementation in order to provide some of the international legal context within which national implementation must operate.

In developing the national legal framework for implementing the Fish Stocks Agreement, however, a wise starting point would seem to be—as it is with the Compliance Agreement—to define what duties the agreement expects the national authorities to carry out and to decide which national authority is to be designated as responsible for doing so.

Designation of General Administrative Authority

It seems highly likely that the national body designated to carry out the national actions and functions that are required to be performed by the national government under the Fish Stocks Agreement will be the same as that designated for the purposes of the Compliance Agreement. This is obviously a matter for national determination, but the designation of this authority and of its responsibilities would normally have to be a part of the national implementing legislation.

One example of this can be found in the draft OECS fisheries law:

This Act shall be administered by the [title] appointed pursuant to [relevant fisheries law] who shall be responsible for:

(1) Issuing fishing permits for fisheries on the high seas in accordance with further rules in chapter [x] of this Act.

(2) Maintaining a record of fishing vessels of [country] in respect of which high seas fishing permits have been issued including all information submitted during the application process.

(3) Maintaining a record of international conservation and management measures and sub-regional or regional fisheries management organizations which are recognized by [country].

(4) Where, following the conclusion of inspection measures in any high seas areas covered by a sub-regional or regional fisheries management organization, in accordance with section [x] of this Act, in respect of a fishing vessel of [country], it is alleged by a foreign State which is Party to the Fish Stocks Agreement that there is clear evidence that an offence has been committed under this Act, the Chief Fisheries Officer may authorize a foreign authorized officer to undertake enforcement measures in respect of that vessel under section [x].

(5) Where, following the conclusion of inspection measures in any high seas areas covered by a sub-regional or regional fisheries management organization, in accordance with section [x] of this Act, in respect of a fishing vessel of [country], it is alleged by a foreign State which is Party to the Fish Stocks Agreement that there is clear evidence that there has been a serious violation of international conservation and management measures [title] may authorize a national authorized officer to undertake enforcement measures in respect of that vessel under section [x].

(6) If [title] has reasonable grounds to believe that a foreign fishing vessel has engaged in activities that undermine the effectiveness of international conservation and management measures, [title]:

(a) shall provide to the appropriate authorities of the flag State of the vessel concerned such information, including evidentiary material, relating to those activities as may be necessary to assist the flag State to identify the vessel;

(b) when such foreign vessel is voluntarily in a port of [country], promptly notify the appropriate authorities of the flag State and, if requested by the flag State make arrangements to undertake such lawful measures as may be considered necessary to establish whether the vessel has been used contrary to the Fish Stocks Agreement.[49]

General Principles in Article 5

Article 5 of the Fish Stocks Agreement sets out the general principles that coastal states and states fishing on the high seas are to apply in order to conserve and manage straddling fish stocks and highly migratory fish stocks. Some of these principles simply restate provisions of the 1982 UN Convention but the agreement also contains elements from other international treaties and various other international instruments adopted since the conclusion of the 1982 UN Convention. These principles apply directly to such measures on the high seas but also, mutatis mutandis, to measures within areas under national jurisdiction.[50]

The Principles. Article 5 contains specific principles on fisheries conservation and management. States that are party to the agreement are to do the following:

- Adopt conservation and management measures to ensure long-term sustainability of straddling fish stocks and highly migratory fish stocks and promote the objective of their optimum utilization;
- Ensure that such measures are based on the best scientific evidence available;
- Apply the precautionary approach;
- Assess the impacts of fishing, other human activities, and environmental factors not only on target stocks but also on species belonging to the same ecosystem or associated with or dependent upon the target stocks; and
- Adopt, where necessary, conservation and management measures for species belonging to the same ecosystem or associated with or dependent on the target stocks.

In addition to these specific principles on fisheries conservation and management, the agreement also includes provisions on minimizing pollution, protecting biodiversity in the marine environment, preventing or eliminating over-fishing and excess fishing capacity, promoting and conducting scientific research, and developing appropriate technologies in support of fishery conservation and management.

National Implementation. Despite the importance of these principles, it is often an issue of national legal drafting "style" as to whether the state implementing legislation specifically enumerates these principles or whether the legal drafter chooses to leave aside the policy dimension and not to implement the general principles of Article 5 in detail into the national legislation.[51] Some nations have taken this latter approach and chosen to give the relevant minister a broad power to implement these principles into national fisheries policy rather than referring to the principles in a law. This approach has been taken in Icelandic legislation implementing the Fish Stocks Agreement, and also in the Namibian Marine Resources Act, 2001.[52]

Parties may, however, decide to implement these principles directly into legislation. An early incorporation of some of these principles into national legislation can be found in the Australian Fisheries Management Act of 1991, which states the following in its section 3 (titled "Objectives"):

(1) The following objectives must be pursued by the Minister in the administration of this Act and by [Australian Fisheries Management Authority] in the performance of its functions:

   . . .

   (b) ensuring that the exploitation of fisheries resources and the carrying on of any related activities are conducted in a manner consistent with the principles of ecologically sustainable development and the exercise of the precautionary principle, in particular the need to have regard to the impact of fishing activities on non-target species and the long term sustainability of the marine environment;

(2) In addition to the objectives mentioned in subsection (1), or in section 78 of this Act, the Minister, AFMA, and the Joint Authorities are to have regard to the objectives of:

   (a) ensuring though proper conservation and management measures, that the living resources of the [Australian Fishing Zone] are not endangered by over-exploitation; and

   (b) achieving the optimum utilisation of the living resources of the AFZ. . .

The following was added by an amendment specifically to give effect to the Fish Stocks Agreement:

> (c) ensuring that conservation and management measures in the AFZ and the high seas implement Australia's obligations under international agreements that deal with fish stocks . . . (Fisheries Legislation Amendment Act, 1999)[53]

A similar approach has been adopted by the Republic of South Africa. Section 2 of the Marine Living Resources Act,[54] which implements both the Compliance Agreement and the Fish Stocks Agreement, is entitled "Objectives and Principles" and reads as follows:

> The Minister and any organ of state shall, in exercising any power under this Act, have regard to the following objectives and principles:
>
> (a) The need to achieve optimum utilization and ecologically sustainable development of marine living resources;
>
> (b) the need to conserve marine living resources for both present and future generations;
>
> (c) the need to apply precautionary approaches in respect of the management and development of marine living resources;
>
> . . .
>
> (e) the need to protect the ecosystem as a whole, including species which are not targeted for exploitation;
>
> (f) the need to preserve marine bio-diversity;
>
> (g) the need to minimize marine pollution;
>
> . . .
>
> (i) any relevant obligation of the national government or the Republic in terms of any international agreement or applicable rule of international law; . . .

Such provisions provide a policy framework for the act and, depending on how they are worded and the local judicial practices concerning judicial review of administrative action, may be enforceable in national courts by means of administrative challenges.[55]

New Zealand also has provided comprehensive provisions setting out broad legal, policy, environmental, and information objectives.

Section 5 of the 1995 Act states the following requirement:

This Act shall be interpreted, and all persons exercising or performing functions, duties, or powers conferred or imposed by or under it shall act, in a manner consistent with—

   (a)   New Zealand's international obligations relating to fishing. . .

Section 8 sets out the following purposes, accompanied by important definitions of key terms that underpin the objectives:

8.   Purpose—(1) The purpose of this Act is to provide for the utilisation of fisheries resources while ensuring sustainability.

(2)   In this Act—

"Ensuring sustainability" means—

   (a)   Maintaining the potential of fisheries resources to meet the reasonably foreseeable needs of future generations; and

   (b)   Avoiding, remedying, or mitigating any adverse effects of fishing on the aquatic environment: "Utilisation" means conserving, using, enhancing, and developing fisheries resources to enable people to provide for their social, economic, and cultural well-being.

The act in a separate section (9) sets out environmental principles as well:

All persons exercising or performing functions, duties, or powers under this Act, in relation to the utilisation of fisheries resources or ensuring sustainability, shall take into account the following environmental principles:

   (a)   Associated or dependent species should be maintained above a level that ensures their long-term viability;

   (b)   Biological diversity of the aquatic environment should be maintained;

   (c)   Habitat of particular significance for fisheries management should be protected.

Finally, section 10 contains information principles:

All persons exercising or performing functions, duties, or powers under this Act, in relation to the utilisation of fisheries resources or ensuring sustainability, shall take into account the following information principles:

   (a)   Decisions should be based on the best available information;

(b) Decision makers should consider any uncertainty in the information available in any case;

(c) Decision makers should be cautious when information is uncertain, unreliable, or inadequate;

(d) The absence of, or any uncertainty in, any information should not be used as a reason for postponing or failing to take any measure to achieve the purpose of this Act.

The New Zealand legislation is interesting in that it breaks down these general objectives into a series of subcategories. In most countries, such objectives are left to more general composite statements.

Canada also has provided for these general principles in its more generally applicable Oceans Act, 1996. Section 29 requires the minister (of Fisheries and Oceans) to lead and facilitate "the development and implementation of a national strategy for the management of estuarine, coastal and marine ecosystems in waters that form part of Canada or in which Canada has sovereign rights under international law." Further, section 30 requires that the:

national strategy will be based on the principles of:

(a) sustainable development, that is, development that meets the needs of the present without compromising the ability of future generations to meet their own needs;

(b) the integrated management of activities in estuaries, coastal waters and marine waters that form part of Canada or in which Canada has sovereign rights under international law; and

(c) the precautionary approach, that is, erring on the side of caution.

Beyond the general principles, the agreement also contains more specific obligations as to the implementation of these principles—for example, the requirements in the general principles that states are to collect and share data on the capture of target and non-target species. In this respect, Article 5 refers to Annex I of the agreement.[56] This annex contains detailed provisions on states' standard requirements for the collection and sharing of data.[57] In order for the owners and operators of vessels to be aware of their duty to supply the government with the necessary information, the requirements for the collection of data need to be implemented into national legislation. This is usually covered in regulations, or as a condition attached to the grant of an authorization to fish. The collection and supply of accurate data on fishing activities is a theme that runs through both the Compliance and Fish Stocks Agreements and is found in other instruments such as the Code of Conduct for Responsible Fisheries and the International Plan of Action on Illegal, Unreported and Unregulated Fishing.

Article 6 on the Precautionary Approach

Article 6 elaborates the precautionary principle, or, as it terms it, "the precautionary approach."[58] This is the first time that precaution has been specifically mentioned in an international fishery convention or applied to straddling and highly migratory stocks.[59] The wording of Article 6 is consistent with the application of the principle pursuant to Agenda 21 and the Rio Declaration. Indeed Principle 15 of the 1992 UNCED Declaration embraces the precautionary approach:

> In order to protect the environment, the precautionary approach shall be widely applied by States according to their capabilities. Where there are threats of serious or irreversible damage, lack of full scientific certainty shall not be used as a reason for postponing cost effective measures to prevent environmental degradation.

Article 6(1) requires that, to preserve the marine environment as well as protect marine living resources, the precautionary approach be applied to the conservation, management, and exploitation of straddling fish stocks and highly migratory fish stocks.[60] It should be noted that the requirement to use precaution in Article 6 does not in itself constitute a reversal of the burden of proof in favor of conservation. The fear of certain fishing states that the acceptance of the precautionary principle would result in the wide-ranging imposition of moratoria was apparent from the discussions at the FAO technical consultations in 1992 as well as the negotiating sessions of the conference. The existing formulation in 6(2) does, however, specify that "states shall be more cautious when information is uncertain, unreliable or inadequate" and that "the absence of adequate scientific information shall not be used as a reason for postponing or failing to take conservation and management measures."[61]

The rest of Article 6, paragraphs 3–7, and Annex II give further details on what these obligations would involve. Article 6(3) sets out the way in which states should implement the precautionary approach. They shall do the following:

(a) improve decision-making for fishery conservation and management by obtaining and sharing the best scientific information available and implementing improved techniques for dealing with risk and uncertainty;

(b) apply the guidelines set out in Annex II and determine, on the basis of the best scientific information available, stock-specific reference points and the action to be taken if they are exceeded;

(c) take into account, inter alia, uncertainties relating to the size and productivity of the stocks, reference points, stock condition in relation to such reference points, levels and distribution of fishing mortality and the impact of fishing activities on non-target and associated or dependent species, as well as existing and predicted oceanic, environmental and socio-economic conditions; and

(d) develop data collection and research programmes to assess the impact of fishing on non-target and associated or dependent species and their environment, and adopt plans which are necessary to ensure the conservation of such species and to protect habitats of special concern.

Paragraphs 5–7 of Article 6 cover special circumstances and emphasize caution and the use of best scientific evidence. Article 6.5 requires enhanced monitoring when the status of target stocks or non-target or associated or dependent species is of concern. Article 6.6 calls for cautious conservation and management measures for new or exploratory fisheries. Finally, Article 6.7 outlines the circumstances in which states should adopt conservation and management measures on an emergency basis.

These requirements, while not reversing the normal burden of proof, do have some considerable impact on the way such issues will be perceived in the future. It is perhaps useful to explore some of the issues involving burden of proof that may arise.

In the past, a key issue of interpretation of a precautionary approach has been whether, in the absence of convincing scientific evidence—that is, using the best scientific evidence available, which may still be unconvincing—

measures should be designed to ensure continued exploitation or to ensure conservation. Should the burden of proof be in favor of exploitation or of conservation? In fisheries, as in areas of environmental monitoring, scientists work on the basis of probabilities. Therefore in cases of scientific uncertainty, if the primary obligation is conservation and maintenance of stocks rather than simple non-sustainable exploitation, then the requirement to utilize the best scientific evidence available appears to be a rule of evidence rather than a standard of proof. Just as the word "best" cannot realistically be taken to mean that evidence for one view or another is intrinsically better, so also it seems difficult to suggest that the word "scientific" is used in a partisan way. It must be correct to say that the word "scientific" means the collection of data according to rigorous objective criteria—which would give data a "minimum standard" requirement. "Availability," however, remains an essentially pragmatic concept. Consequently, if adequate evidence is simply not available the general obligations of the convention still remain, and the primary applicable obligation is that of conservation.

Nevertheless, the significance of precaution should not be underrated. There is now an obligation on state parties to be cautious and to utilize the procedures set out in Annex II. This represents a major change in the traditional approach of fisheries management, which until recently has tended to react to management problems only after they reached crisis levels.[62] The new regime will allow fishing states and regional and international fisheries organizations to justify proactive measures more easily; indeed, from now on such measures should be built into the system. Stock management standards must also be handled in a precautionary manner, taking into account such factors as uncertainties relating to size and productivity of fish stocks; levels and distribution of fish mortality; and the impact of fishing activities on associated or dependent species, including existing and predicted oceanic, environmental, and socioeconomic conditions.[63]

The application of the precautionary approach to capture fisheries represents a real challenge.[64] The precautionary methodology in the agreement centers on the use of reference points. The reference points identified as necessary to ensure the conservation and management of species are to be based on the data collection and research programs referred to in Article 6(3)(d) and the Guidelines for the Application of Precautionary Reference Points in Conservation and Management of Straddling Fish Stocks and Highly Migratory

Fish Stocks set out in Annex II of the agreement. The specificity of the language of Annex II and the variety of circumstances to which it could theoretically apply give reason for optimism that the Annex II regime will be a significant improvement on existing comparable regimes from a conservation and management perspective. It has to be said, however, that the agreement does not clarify the implications of exceeding reference points; these issues, together with the setting of reference points themselves, are left to states acting through regional fisheries organizations.[65]

In relation to the establishment of precautionary reference points, Annex II also leaves a great deal to be determined by the relevant regional fisheries regulatory body. A number of authors have developed theoretical frameworks for precautionary approaches to capture fisheries.[66] The agreement does provide a basic methodology for addressing most of the key issues, including action to be taken in the absence of sufficient data,[67] a scientifically based management procedure,[68] calculation of reference stock levels,[69] ecological safeguards,[70] and participatory and open decision making.[71] Further work has also been done by FAO and the Swedish National Fisheries Board. Together, they formulated the Guidelines on the Precautionary Approach to Capture Fisheries,[72] which develops a management approach compatible with the provisions of the agreement.

National Implementation of the Precautionary Approach. As with other general principles of the agreement, it is left to the discretion of each state party to determine how it will implement the precautionary approach. At this moment it is hard to speculate exactly how nations will choose to implement the approach on a national level since most nations that have already implemented the agreement have decided not to implement it directly into national legislation, preferring to do so through national policy. It is quite possible for a state to give full effect to this approach without it being referred to any legislative instrument, provided that the end result yields the same level of precaution.[73] For example, regulations concerning conservation measures might merely refer to certain closed areas or seasons or catch rates in a way that is precautionary in effect because the basic information concerning a fishery is "uncertain, unreliable, or inaccurate." However, this may not be mentioned in the regulations, and indeed, in a number of countries in the common law world, it would run counter to established drafting traditions to make such a reference.

As we have seen above however, laws in Australia and South Africa do contain explicit references to the obligation to apply the precautionary approach.

Another instance in which the precautionary approach is implicitly acknowledged is in the Namibian Marine Resources Act in its provisions dealing with an exploratory fishing right. It should be mentioned that in addition to this provision, which is set out below, it would still be possible for the government to introduce or apply precautionary measures through the formulation of policy, license issues, regulations, and so on, even without using that term. What makes the provision below of more general interest is that it is clearly underpinned by the basic objective of the precautionary approach.

Exploratory right to harvest marine resources

34. (1) The Minister may grant a single exploratory right to harvest any marine resource for which no right has been granted or to use any method of harvesting the commercial viability and biological sustainability of which has not been established.

   (2) A person who wishes to apply for an exploratory right shall submit an application to the Minister in the manner prescribed, and may do so at any time.

   (3) The Minister may require the applicant to carry out or cause to be carried out such environmental impact studies as the Minister may consider necessary for the purposes of this Act or any other law.

   (4) The Minister may approve the application and grant an exploratory right for such fixed period and subject to such conditions, including permitted by-catch, as may be determined by the Minister, or may refuse the application.

   (5) Upon the expiry of an exploratory right, the Minister shall determine whether the resource or method of harvesting is commercially viable and biologically sustainable, and if he or she determines that it is, no further exploratory right may be granted in respect of that resource or method of harvesting.

   (6) In the event that the commercial viability and biological sustainability of the resource or method of harvesting is unclear, the Minister may extend the exploratory right once only for a period not exceeding one year or, if the commercial viability and biological sustainabil-

ity are unclear due to the poor execution of the exploratory right, a further exploratory right may be granted to an applicant other than the holder of the original exploratory right.

(7) If before the end of the term of an exploratory right it becomes clear that the resource or method of harvesting is commercially viable and biologically sustainable, the Minister may terminate the exploratory right and announce a period during which applications for rights may be made under section 33(1).

Even though some state parties may choose not to implement the precautionary approach directly into their legislation, they still have an obligation to be cautious and follow the procedures set out in Annex II. This represents a major change in traditional fisheries management, which until recently has tended to be reactive instead of proactive.

Article 7: Cooperation and Compatibility on the High Seas and within the EEZ

Article 7(2) of the Fish Stocks Agreement obliges states that are party to the agreement to develop conservation and management measures for straddling fish stocks and highly migratory fish stocks, that are compatible for the high seas and their EEZ. Because these fish stocks, which straddle from one jurisdiction to another, suffer from "being the subject of competing and potentially conflicting rules: those established by one or more coastal states to govern the stock in the EEZ(s), and those adopted multilaterally by coastal and fishing states to govern the stock on the high seas."[74] To achieve sound management of these fish stocks, states therefore need to cooperate on managing the stocks as a whole—which is precisely the purpose of Article 7.

Article 7 tries to balance the interests of coastal states and DWFS and "reduce or eliminate conflicts that may arise between measures taken within an EEZ and those which apply in the adjacent high seas area through a strategy based on cooperation."[75]

Article 7(1) makes a distinction between the conservation and management measures that the state parties shall seek to agree or cooperate upon for straddling fish stocks on one hand and highly migratory fish stocks on the other. While the measures for the highly migratory fish stocks are to apply to the high seas as well as to the EEZ, the measures for the straddling fish stocks shall only apply to the high seas.[76] This restates the distinction between these stocks that is to be found in Articles 63(2) and 64 of the 1982 UN Convention.

The basic obligation to achieve compatibility is stated in Article 7(2):

> Conservation and management measures established for the high seas and those adopted for areas under national jurisdiction shall be compatible in order to ensure conservation and management of the straddling fish stocks and highly migratory fish stocks in their entirety. To this end, coastal States and States fishing on the high seas have a duty to cooperate for the purpose of achieving compatible measures in respect of such stocks.[77]

In determining compatible conservation and management measures, states shall take into account a variety of factors detailed in Article 7(2)(a)–(e) and ensure that such measures do not result in any "harmful impact on the living marine resources as a whole."[78] The factors that states are to take into consideration include the extent to which stocks are found and fished for in areas under national jurisdiction, the biological unity and characteristics of fish stocks, and "the respective dependence of the coastal states and the states fishing on the high seas on the stocks concerned."

According to Article 7(3), "States shall make every effort to agree on compatible conservation and management measures within a reasonable period of time." If no agreement can be reached within that time period, Article 7(4) allows any of the states concerned to invoke the procedures for the settlement of disputes provided for in part VIII of the agreement.

Pending agreement on compatible conservation and management measures, Article 7(5)–(6) calls on states to develop provisional arrangements to achieve compatibility. If states are not able to reach an agreement on such provisional arrangements, any state concerned may invoke additional dispute settlement procedures for establishing provisional measures.

Article 7 does not call for any implementation into national law before ratifying the agreement. States may, however, wish to implement into national law the basic duty to cooperate in this respect. That has been done in the United States with regard to highly migratory fish stocks. Section 102 of the Fishery Conservation and Management Act, entitled "Highly Migratory Species," implements the duty of the United States to cooperate "directly or through appropriate international organizations with those nations involved in fisheries for highly migratory species [to ensure] conservation and . . . promote the achievement of optimum yield of such species throughout their range, both within and beyond the exclusive economic zone."

By ratifying the agreement, parties do commit themselves to certain modalities of international cooperation, specified above, the results of which they may need to implement into national legislation. As for fisheries on the high seas, states will typically work together through regional fishery organizations or similar bodies that must observe the obligations of Article 7 and will presumably have a strong influence on their conservation and management measures.

Parts III and IV

Articles 8–17 in part III of the agreement relate entirely to the mechanisms for international cooperation concerning measures RFOs need to take at the international level toward the conservation and management of straddling fish stocks and highly migratory fish stocks, and Article 17 in part IV relates to the issue of non-members of RFOs and non-participants in other fishery arrangements. While national drafters will need to be aware of these dimensions of the Fish Stocks Agreement, they relate primarily to the rights and duties of states at the international level and require little, if any, implementation at the national level. Implementation and compliance with the conservation and management measures agreed on by those bodies will of course require extensive national powers.

Regional Fisheries Organizations

The Fish Stocks Agreement lays down the basic legal framework for the conservation and management of straddling fish stocks and highly migratory fish stocks; however, it calls for RFOs to adopt detailed measures. Part III, Articles 8–16 of the agreement provide guidelines for the establishment of regional fisheries organizations and a clarification of their enforcement powers. RFOs play an important role in implementing the agreement. Effective implementation of the agreement at the regional level is the only way for nations to ensure that the straddling fish stocks and highly migratory fish stocks that partly live within their EEZ are conserved and managed in a holistic way.[79]

Duty to Cooperate

To ensure effective conservation and management of straddling and highly migratory fish stocks, all states that are party to the agreement must, in accordance with Article 8(1), pursue cooperation to this end either directly or through an appropriate RFO. Article 8(3) obliges states to give effect to their duty to cooperate in managing these fish stocks by participating in RFO measures. However, only those states that have a "real interest" in the fisheries concerned may become members of such an organization. Article 8(4) further provides that only those states that participate in or abide by the measures of the relevant RFOs shall have access to the fishery in the RFOs' regulatory area. This introduces a new and "important restriction on the concept of freedom of fishing on the high seas."[80]

Structure and Function

Articles 9–12 of the agreement detail the structure and function of future RFOs. They are to be established in conjunction with an agreement among relevant fishing parties on such factors as the stock(s) and area to which the measures are to apply, and the mechanisms by which the RFOs will obtain scientific advice. Moreover, RFOs are to be the forum for parties to establish, and abide by, procedures concerning scientific measurement, monitoring, control, surveillance, and enforcement mechanisms.[81]

Collection and Exchange of Data

Accurate data are fundamental to any effective management system. To advance the effectiveness of fishery management efforts, Article 14 calls for the collection and exchange of scientific data. Article 14(1) requires that, in implementing Annex I, states must collect and exchange "sufficiently detailed" data relating to straddling and highly migratory fish stocks in a timely manner. Although the agreement itself does not lay down any criteria for assessing sufficiency in this regard, Article 14(2) does go on to call upon states to work together, through subregional or regional fisheries organizations or arrangements, in developing standards on data specification, analytical techniques, stock assessment methodologies, and scientific research capacity.[82]

National Implementation

The formation, membership, or function of RFOs does not call for any national implementation. The duty to cooperate with RFOs and adhere to their conservation and management measures does, however, oblige the vessels and nationals of the state parties to comply with these measures. The modalities for doing this are discussed extensively below, but at a general level compliance with the conservation and management measures of designated RFOs could be a condition for receiving a permit to fish on the high seas. There are a number of ways in which this could be implemented into national legislation. One is by giving the relevant minister the power to add conditions to the fishing permit to comply with international conservation and management measures. This is the approach taken by the Canadian legislation. Section 6 of the Canadian Coastal Fisheries Protection Act[83] reads as follows:

> The Governor in council may make regulations for carrying out the purposes and provisions of this Act including, but not limited to, regulations . . .
>
> (e) for the implementation of the [Fish Stocks] Agreement, including regulations
>
> > (i) incorporating by reference any conservation or management measures of a regional fisheries management organization or arrangement established by two or more States, or by one or more States and an organization of States, for the purpose of the conservation or management of a straddling fish stock or highly migratory fish stock . . .

Part V: Duties of the Flag State

Part V, Article 18, of the Fish Stocks Agreement outlines the duties of the flag states that are parties to the agreement. It maintains the basic concept of flag state responsibility over vessels fishing on the high seas and outlines detailed provisions on the specific obligations which a flag state must agree to and implement before its nationals are permitted to fish on the high seas and in areas managed by RFOs.

It is perhaps important to point out at the outset that this provision appears not to be limited to vessels engaged in fishing for straddling fish stocks and highly migratory fish stocks, but to apply to all vessels fishing on the high seas. Article 18(1) reads as follows: "A State whose vessels fish on the high seas shall take such measures. . . ." There is no qualification that these vessels should be fishing for straddling fish stocks or highly migratory fish stocks.[84]

At the outset, therefore, it will be necessary for national law to identify clearly those vessels that are subject to the control of the flag state in order for the flag state to exercise effectively the duties adumbrated in Article 18. This will usually require in the applicable legislation a definition of such vessels. An example can be found from Australia, which introduced legislation to give effect to its obligations under the Fish Stocks Agreement and inserted the following definition into its legislation:

> [An] "Australian-flagged boat" means a boat that:
> (a) is an Australian ship as defined in the Shipping Registration Act 1981; or
> (b) would be an Australian ship as defined in the Shipping Registration Act 1981 if it were a ship as defined in that Act.[85]

Article 18(1) states the basic obligation that flag states have to fulfill in accordance with the agreement. Flag states are to make sure that the vessels flying their flags and fishing on the high seas comply with subregional and regional conservation and management measures and do not undermine the effectiveness of those measures. Although this is a duty the state party itself undertakes—in other words, taking such measures as may be necessary to ensure the behavior of vessels flying its flag—it can only carry out this duty effectively through national legal measures that both criminalize the activity and provide penalties for violation. Exactly which detailed measures vessels are required to comply with would be defined from time to time by the relevant RFO.

Indeed, Article 18(2) of the Fish Stocks Agreement goes further than this and provides that flag states are not to authorize their vessels to fish on the high seas unless they are sure that they are able to exercise their responsibilities in accordance with the agreement and the 1982 UN Convention. In this respect the Fish Stocks Agreement is similar to the Compliance Agreement, but the former goes on to make this duty even more explicit in Article 18(3)–(4).

Further Measures that States Are to Take with Regard to Vessels Flying Their Flags and Fishing on the High Seas

1. States are to establish a national record of fishing vessels authorized to fish on the high seas and provide access to the information contained in that record on request by directly interested states, taking into account any national laws of the flag state regarding the release of such information (Article 18(3)(c)).

2. States are to require their fishing vessels and gear to be marked for identification in accordance with uniform and internationally recognizable vessel and gear marking systems, such as FAO's Standard Specifications for the Marking and Identification of Fishing Vessels (Article 18(3)(d)).

3. States are to require recording and timely reporting of vessel position, catch of target and non-target species, fishing effort, and other relevant fisheries data in accordance with subregional, regional, and global standards for collection of such data from fishing vessels (Article 18(3)(e)).

4. States shall verify the catch of target and non-target species through such means as observer programs, inspection schemes, unloading reports, supervision of transshipment, and monitoring of landed catches and market statistics (Article 18(3)(f)).

5. States shall establish monitoring, control, and surveillance of their fishing vessels fishing on the high seas, their fishing operations, and related activities (Article 18(3)(g)).

6. States shall regulate transshipment on the high seas to ensure that the effectiveness of conservation and management measures is not undermined (Article 18(3)(h)).

7. States shall regulate fishing activities to ensure compliance with subregional, regional, or global measures, including those aimed at minimizing catches of non-target species (Article 18(3)(i)).

8. States shall ensure that the national system of monitoring, control, and surveillance is compatible with the subregionally, regionally, or globally agreed system, if any, in effect (Article 18(4)).

According to Article 18(3), states need to take the following measures to discharge properly their responsibility for vessels flying their flag:

(a) control of such vessels on the high seas flying their flags by means of fishing licenses, authorizations or permits in accordance with any applicable procedures agreed at the sub-regional, regional or global level.[86]

(b) establishment of regulations detailing these measures. These regulations should:

   (i)   apply terms and conditions to the licence, authorization or permit sufficient to fulfil any sub-regional, regional or global obligations of the flag State;

   (ii) prohibit fishing on the high seas by vessels which are not duly licensed or authorized to fish, or fishing on the high seas by vessels otherwise than in accordance with the terms and conditions of a licence, authorization or permit;

   (iii) require vessels fishing on the high seas to carry the licence, authorization or permit on board at all times and to produce it on demand for inspection by a duly authorized person; and

   (iv) ensure that vessels flying its flag do not conduct unauthorized fishing within areas under the national jurisdiction of other States.[87]

Implementation into National Law

Registration of Fishing Vessels and Issuance of Licenses

In 1997 FAO collaborated with the Organization of Eastern Caribbean States[88] to put together a workshop on the implementation of the two agreements. Attached to the report of the meeting is draft legislation that follows the commonwealth common law style. In the introduction to the draft, the legal drafters suggest that "while the basic principles, provisions for licensing, boarding and inspections, etc. will need to be included in primary legislation, much of the detail will have to be left to regulations as any monitoring, control and surveillance measures will have to be compatible with measures agreed at the subregional, regional and global levels."[89] The OECS draft then gives the following detailed version of how these duties of the flag state might be implemented into national legislation. Although long, it is worth reproducing in full:

Regulation of Fishing in Areas beyond National Jurisdiction.

5. (1) No fishing vessel of [country] shall be used for fishing or related activities on the high seas unless the vessel has on board a valid high seas fishing permit.

. . .

6. (1) The owner, charterer or operator of a fishing vessel of [country] may apply for a high seas fishing permit in respect of that vessel by completing an application in a form prescribed by the Minister. The application form shall contain details of:

   (a) the vessel's name, previous names (if known), registration numbers and port of registry;

   (b) the vessel's previous flags (if any);

   (c) the vessel's International Radio Call Sign (if any);

   (d) the names and addresses of the vessels' owners and operators;

   (e) where and when the vessel was built;

   (f) the type of vessel;

   (g) the vessel's length;

   (h) the type of fishing method or methods;

   (i) the moulded depth of the vessel;

   (j) the beam of the vessel;

   (k) the gross register tonnage of the vessel;

   (l) the power of the main engine or engines of the vessel;

   (m) vessel navigation and position fixing equipment; and

   (n) any other information the Minister requires for the purpose of implementing the . . . Fish Stocks Agreement, or for the purpose of giving effect to international conservation and management measures.

   (2) The Minister shall have regard to the following matters in determining whether or not to grant a high seas fishing permit:

   (a) the capacity of [country] to implement its obligations under the Compliance Agreement and the Fish Stocks Agreement;

   (b) the advice of the Chief Fisheries Officer;

   (c) the previous conduct of the person or persons applying for the permit; and

   (d) any other relevant matter.

(3) The Minister shall not issue a high seas fishing permit in respect of a vessel unless the Minister is satisfied that [country] will be able to exercise effectively its responsibilities under the Compliance Agreement, the Fish Stocks Agreement and international conservation and management measures with respect to that vessel.

. . .

7. The Minister shall, by notice published in the Gazette, determine the level of fees payable for a high seas fishing permit and in setting the level of any such fees the minister shall have due regard to the fisheries management costs of [country] in fulfilling its obligations under international law.

8. (1) Every high seas fishing permit shall be in the prescribed form and shall contain the following conditions:

    (a) the vessel to which the permit relates shall be marked in accordance with Regulations issued under section [XX] of the Fisheries Act 19XX;

    (b) the vessel shall not engage in any activities which undermine the effectiveness of international conservation and management measures; and

    (c) the permit holder shall report such information as the Minister requires, including the area of fishing operations, vessel position and catch statistics.

(2) The Minister may attach such other conditions and restrictions to each high seas fishing permit as are necessary and appropriate to carry out the obligations of [country] under the Compliance Agreement and the Fish Stocks Agreement, including, but not limited to, the following:

    (a) the area or areas in which fishing is authorised;

    (b) the period, times or particular voyages during which fishing is authorised;

    (c) the descriptions, quantities, size and presentation of fish which may be taken;

    (d) the method of fishing to be undertaken;

    (e) the marking of gear;

    (f) a requirement that the vessel carry observers on board during fishing operations on the high seas;

(g)   a requirement that access be permitted to foreign observers;

(h)   a requirement that additional monitoring equipment be carried;

(i)   measures to be taken to avoid catching non-target species;

(j)   requirements for recording and timely reporting of vessel position, catch of target and non-target species, fishing effort and other relevant fisheries data;

(k)   requirements for verifying the catch of target and non-target species; and

(l)   the stowage of gear.

(3)   The Minister may vary any conditions attached to a high seas fishing permit where the Minister is satisfied that this is necessary to ensure compliance by [country] with its obligations under the Compliance Agreement or the Fish Stocks Agreement.

(4)   Where the Minister varies any conditions attached to a high seas fishing permit the Minister shall notify the permit holder of such variation as soon as practicable.

(5)   Where a fishing vessel of [country] is used in contravention of any condition or restriction contained in the high seas fishing permit the master, owner charter or operator of the vessel shall each be guilty of an offence and shall be liable on summary conviction to a fine. . . .

9.   (1)   A high seas fishing permit is valid for one year or such other period as may be specified in the permit.

   (2)   A high seas fishing permit is void in the event that the vessel in respect of which it was granted is no longer entitled to fly the flag of [country].

10.   (1)   The Minister may cancel or suspend a high seas fishing permit where the Minister is satisfied that:

   (a)   the vessel in respect of which the permit was granted has been used in contravention of this Act or any regulations made pursuant to this Act or in breach of any conditions or restrictions in the permit;

   (b)   the vessel in respect of which the permit was granted has engaged in activities undermining the effectiveness of international conservation and management measures; or

> (c)   it is necessary to ensure compliance by [country] with its oblig-
> ations under the Compliance Agreement, the Fish Stocks
> Agreement or international conservation and management
> measures.
>
> (2)   At the same time as canceling or suspending a permit, the Minister
> may also direct that the vessel in respect of which the permit was
> granted return immediately to port.
>
> (3)   If a permit is cancelled or suspended the Minister may, taking into
> account the circumstances of the case, refund the whole or part of
> any fee charged for the permit.

The distinctive approach of the OECS draft is to include all these details in the primary legislation itself—with limited powers of ministerial discretion. Other states might of course choose to implement these details in part through delegated legislation such as through regulations.

An alternative approach is to be found in New Zealand, which introduced in 1999 a comprehensive amendment to the pre-existing 1996 Fisheries Act, dealing with these detailed issues.[90] The 1999 amendment adds a new part 6A, on high seas fishing, to the 1996 act. Section 113d of the new provisions contains a blanket prohibition on the use by any person of a New Zealand ship or a tender of that ship to take, on the high seas, any fish, aquatic life, or seaweed for sale *unless* (a) this is done under the authority of, and in accordance with, a high seas fishing permit issued in respect of that ship; (b) the ship is registered under the Ship Registration Act and in the fishing vessel register as a fishing vessel; and (c) the holder of the permit is named in the register as an operator of that vessel. A similar prohibition is made in respect of transporting any fish and the like.[91]

Further provisions (too detailed to set out here) relating to the issuance of a high seas fishing permit have been included in the amendment. These include provisions concerning the non-issuance of a fishing permit in cases in which the person in question has engaged in fishing or transportation in a manner that has undermined international conservation and management measures and that has resulted in the suspension of a fishing authorization by a participating state in the conservation and management measures or by a party to the Compliance Agreement.[92]

One part that is worth quoting in full in these New Zealand provisions is the range of conditions that may be imposed in respect of the issuance of a high seas fishing permit.

113K. *Conditions of high seas fishing permit—*

(1) A high seas fishing permit may be subject to such conditions as the chief executive considers appropriate, including conditions relating to the following matters:

(a) The areas in which fishing or transportation is authorised;

(b) The seasons, times, and particular voyages during which fishing or transportation is authorised;

(c) The species, size, age, and quantities of fish, aquatic life, or seaweed that may be taken or transported;

(d) The methods by which fish, aquatic life, or seaweed may be taken;

(e) The types, size, and amount of fishing gear or equipment that may be used or carried, and the modes of storage of that gear or equipment when not in use;

(f) The use, transfer, transshipment, landing, receiving, and processing of fish, aquatic life, or seaweed taken;

(g) Procedures or requirements, or both, enabling the verification of fish, aquatic life, or seaweed taken or being taken by the vessel, including procedures or restrictions relating to the species of, quantities of, or areas from which fish, aquatic life, or seaweed are being or have been taken by the vessel;

(h) Entry by the vessel to New Zealand or foreign ports, whether for the inspection of its catch or for other purposes;

(i) Reports and information required to be given to the chief executive by the permit holder, and records required to be kept by the permit holder;

(j) Management controls regarding fishing-related mortality of fish, aquatic life, or seaweed;

(k) The conduct of specified programmes of fisheries research;

(l) The marking of the vessel and other means for its identification;

(m) The placing of observers on the vessel and the payment of any associated prescribed fees and charges by the permit holder;

(n)   The installation and maintenance of equipment to monitor fishing or transportation under the permit and the payment of any associated prescribed fees and charges by the permit holder;

(o)   The installation on the vessel and the maintenance of any automatic location communicator or other equipment for the identification and location of the vessel, and of adequate navigational equipment to enable the vessel to fix its position, and the payment of any associated prescribed fees and charges by the permit holder;

(p)   The carriage on board the vessel of specified charts, publications, and instruments;

(q)   The disposal of fish, aquatic life, and seaweed;

(r)   Measures to give effect to international conservation and management measures.

Other Duties of Flag States

The duties imposed on the flag state as set out in the Fish Stocks Agreement will require some considerable additional legislation to give effect to them in full. Following is a description of how some of the more interesting provisions have been addressed.

The novel provisions concerning international cooperation in enforcement, subregional and regional cooperation in enforcement, and basic procedures for boarding and inspection usually will require detailed legislative attention, especially in common law countries.

Compliance and Enforcement

The provisions concerning compliance and enforcement raise many novel points; owing to space constraints we will refer to only a few of the more novel ones here that merit specific legislative implementation. Article 19 of the Fish Stocks Agreement requires that the flag state ensure compliance by vessels flying its flag. This provision sets out the general obligations of the flag state, while the subsequent articles (Articles 20–22) deal with international compliance and enforcement. The basic approach of the agreement is to oblige flag states to enforce subregional and regional conservation and management measures for straddling fish stocks and highly migratory fish stocks not only against their own vessels (that is, vessels flying their flag) but against all vessels and *wherever* they may be—within their own waters, on the high seas, or in the waters of another state.[93]

Furthermore—and most significantly for the legislator—the agreement authorizes state parties to board and inspect vessels flying the flags of other state parties in any high seas area covered by a subregional or regional fisheries management organization or agreement.[94] These organizations and arrangements should establish agreed-upon boarding and inspection procedures for such circumstances,[95] but if within two years of the "adoption" of the agreement no specific procedures have been established by these bodies, such boarding and inspection activities may be allowed to take place in accordance with the detailed requirements of Articles 20 and 21. If such an inspection reveals that there are "clear grounds for believing that the vessel has engaged in an activity contrary to applicable conservation and management measures," then the inspecting state must secure evidence and must notify the flag state promptly of the alleged violation.[96] The flag state, which must have designated an appropriate authority to receive such notifications,[97] must respond within three working days and must either take enforcement action itself or authorize the inspecting state to proceed with an investigation and, if appropriate, may authorize the inspecting state to take enforcement action against its vessel.[98]

The implementation of these provisions is a considerable challenge. It requires the legislator to envisage situations in which vessels flying its flag are the offenders, as well as other situations in which they are vessels of an inspecting state. The law will also require many countries to introduce amendments to existing legislation to ensure that the existing enforcement powers can be applied in novel situations. For example, Article 19.1(a) requires the flag state to enforce subregional and regional conservation and management measures *wherever* they occur. This poses an unusual, although not unprecedented, situation for those countries, in particular those with a common law tradition, where legislation is assumed not to operate extraterritorially unless the legislation clearly indicates that it is intended to do so.

More generally, the legislation will also need to ensure that measures are taken to ensure that a vessel that has committed a "serious violation"[99] does not engage in fishing operations on the high seas until such time as all outstanding sanctions imposed by the flag state in respect of the violation have been complied with. This obligation has its parallel in the Compliance Agreement.

New Zealand has a common law tradition; there is a general presumption against extraterritoriality. Therefore it is of some interest to see the way that the New Zealand legislation has given effect to the obligations found in these important new provisions. Extraterritoriality is addressed at the outset by the inclusion of the following clause:

198A. To avoid doubt, the powers of a fishery officer conferred by or under this Part may be exercised in relation to any conduct, whether or not the conduct occurred in New Zealand fisheries waters.

The substantive provisions of the New Zealand amendments are reproduced at length below because they demonstrate vividly how the interlocking provisions of Articles 19–22 can be synthesized into one inspection scheme applicable to both national and foreign vessels:

113Q. *High seas fishery inspectors*
(1)   Every fishery officer (other than an honorary fishery officer or an examiner) is a high seas fishery inspector.
(2)   A high seas fishery inspector may direct a person under his or her command to carry out such duties of a high seas fishery inspector as he or she specifies, for such period as he or she thinks necessary.
(3)   A person who receives a direction under subsection (2) has, for the purpose of carrying out the specified duties, all the powers of a high seas fishery inspector.

113R. *Powers of high seas fishery inspectors in relation to New Zealand vessels*—For the purposes of the administration and enforcement of this Part, a high seas fishery inspector has all of the powers of a fishery officer in relation to a vessel on the high seas that—
(a)   Is registered under the Ship Registration Act 1992; or
(b)   Flies the New Zealand flag.

113S. *Powers of high seas fishery inspectors in relation to foreign vessels*—
(1)   A high seas fishery inspector may, for the purpose of ensuring compliance with international conservation and management measures adopted by a global, regional, or sub-regional fisheries organisation or

arrangement of which New Zealand is a member or in which New Zealand is a participant, board and inspect a vessel in an area of the high seas that is covered by that organisation or arrangement, or in New Zealand fisheries waters, if—

(a)   The vessel is not registered under the Ship Registration Act 1992; and

(b)   The flag state of the vessel is—

   (i)   A party to the Fish Stocks Agreement, whether or not the flag state is a member of, or a participant in, that organisation or arrangement; or

   (ii)   A member of, or participant in, a global, regional, or sub-regional organisation or arrangement that has established boarding and inspection procedures as provided in Article 21.2 of the Fish Stocks Agreement.

(2)   If the flag state in relation to a vessel to which sub-section (1) applies authorises the chief executive (in accordance with Article 21.6 (b) of the Fish Stocks Agreement) to investigate whether the vessel has engaged in an activity contrary to those international conservation and management measures, a high seas fishery inspector has, in relation to the vessel—

(a)   All of the powers of a fishery officer; or

(b)   If the flag state specifies the powers of a fishery officer that the high seas fishery inspector may exercise, those powers.

Section 113T deals with boarding and inspection procedures relating to foreign vessels, and section 113U deals with investigation of serious violations. Section 113U is also worth quoting in full :

113U. *Investigation of serious violations*—

(1)   If, as a result of a boarding and inspection under section 113S (1), a high seas fishery inspector believes that the vessel has been used to commit a serious violation—

(a)   The high seas fishery inspector must notify the chief executive as soon as practicable; and

(b)   The chief executive must advise the authorities of the flag state of the vessel as soon as practicable.

(2)   A high seas fishery inspector may remain on board the vessel and may require the master to assist in further investigations for so long as the flag state—

(a)   Fails to respond to a notification under subsection (1); or

(b)   Fails to take action under its own law in respect of the serious violation.

(3)   The high seas fishery inspector may require the master to bring the vessel without delay to a port specified by the high seas fishery inspector if the flag state fails, within 3 working days after receipt by the authorities of the flag state of the notification, to—

(a)   Respond to a notification under subsection (1); or

(b)   Take action under its own law in respect of the serious violation.

Section 113V provides for the application of boarding and inspection procedures in cases in which they have been modified by a global, regional, or subregional organization or arrangement, in which event the procedures in section 113T and section 113U are modified to the extent needed.

Section 113W places an obligation on persons on New Zealand ships to cooperate with foreign high seas inspectors.

The amendment continues:

113X. *Powers of foreign high seas inspector when requested to investigate*

(1)   The chief executive may authorise a foreign high seas inspector to investigate a ship that is registered under the Ship Registration Act 1992 or that flies the New Zealand flag, under Article 21.6 (b) of the Fish Stocks Agreement, if—

(a)   The inspector has boarded the ship under—

(i)   The Agreement; or

(ii)   Boarding and inspection procedures established as provided in Article 21.2 of the Agreement; and

(b)   The chief executive receives a report from the inspector stating that there is evidence that the ship has taken or transported fish, aquatic life, or seaweed in contravention of international conservation and management measures.

(2)   If the chief executive authorises the foreign high seas inspector to investigate under Article 21.6 (b) of the Fish Stocks Agreement;

(a) The foreign high seas inspector has the powers of a fishery officer in relation to the ship; and

(b) The chief executive must advise the master of the ship as soon as practicable.

(3) For the purposes of any proceedings for an offence under this Part, evidence obtained by a foreign high seas inspector in the exercise of powers under this section is admissible as if the evidence were obtained by a fishery officer.

The approach taken by the Australian legislation is also to amend existing legislation but to approach the task on a more piecemeal basis. Hence they are not as easily quoted as the New Zealand text as they are in effect clause-by-clause amendments to the specific clauses of the pre-existing 1991 Fisheries Management Act. It is worth exploring a little, however, the way that this has been done.

With regard to the exercise of the important new enforcement powers on the high seas, this power has been granted by an extensive amendment of section 84 of the 1991 act relating to the "Powers of Officers." Thus the powers of officers in respect of so-called Fish Stocks Agreement boats (that is, boats flying the flag of states that are party to the 1995 agreement) on the high seas implement specifically Article 20.6 of the agreement.[100] This has been achieved by the following amendment:

87A *Officers' powers: FSA boat on high seas after illegally fishing in AFZ*[101]

(1) Paragraphs 84(1)(aa), (a), (c), (n), (o), (p) and (r) apply in relation to an FSA boat on the high seas in the same way as they apply in relation to a boat in the AFZ, if the officer mentioned in subsection 84(1) has reasonable grounds to believe that:

(a) the boat has been used in the AFZ or Australia or an external Territory in contravention of section 95; and

(b) the boarding of the boat has been authorised by the appropriate authority of the country of nationality of the boat.

Another amendment provides for the powers of officers in respect of "Fish Stocks Agreement boats" fishing on the high seas and is aimed at implementing Articles 21 and 22 of the 1995 agreement. The amendments are very extensive indeed, and it is enough to refer to the explanatory memorandum as to what was intended by the extremely lengthy amendment:

> This Clause [87B] implements Articles 21 and 22 of the Agreement which provides a right for non-flag State (the inspecting State) boarding and inspection on the high sea. Foreign boats with a nationality of parties to the Fish Stocks Agreement may be boarded and inspected for the purposes of checking compliance with regional management measures. The Agreement provides a prescribed boarding and inspection process to protect the interests of the fishing boat and the inspecting State. The prescribed boarding and inspection process is implemented through modification of the present powers of fisheries officers (in section 84 of the Act). The inspecting State is initially limited to powers that may be used to *inspect*. Following an inspection, further powers may be exercised to *investigate* (including taking a boat to the nearest appropriate port) when either:
>
> (a) there is grounds for believing the boat has contravened a regional management measure and the flag State has authorised the inspecting State to undertake further investigation; or
>
> (b) a serious violation has been committed and the flag State fails to respond by undertaking to conduct their own investigation or authorizing the inspecting State.[102]

Similarly, provision is made for the powers of inspecting officers in respect of a "Fish Stocks Agreement boat" in Australian waters. This is aimed at giving effect to Article 21(14) of the 1995 agreement,[103] and is achieved by the following amendment:

> (1) This section operates in relation to an FSA boat in the AFZ, Australia or an external Territory, but only if:
>
>   (a) the FSA boat is equipped for fishing; and
>
>   (b) an officer has reasonable grounds to believe that the boat is on a fishing trip within the meaning of the Fish Stocks Agreement; and
>
>   (c) the officer has reasonable grounds to believe that, in the course of the fishing trip:
>
>   (i) the boat has been used on the high seas in contravention of an Australian regional management measure; and
>
>   (ii) the boat entered the AFZ after the contravention.[104]

Other amendments provide for the officer's powers to continue when a boat with the nationality of a party to the Fish Stocks Agreement is at a place in a foreign country or in the EEZ, territorial sea, archipelagic waters, or internal waters of a foreign country (section 87D), as well as provide limits on the exercise of powers in respect of such boats as provided for under Article 21 of the agreement (section 87E).

The basic boarding and inspection procedures in Article 22 of the 1995 agreement discussed above have been implemented into section 87F of the 1999 Australian legislation in the following manner:

Overview

(1)   This section applies if an officer on an FSA boat exercises powers under section 84 as it applies because of section 87B, 87C or 87D.

Showing documents to master

(2)   When, or as soon as practicable after, an officer first exercises a power on the boat relating to an offence against section 105E or 105F in relation to an Australian regional management measure, an officer must show the master of the boat:

   (a)   a copy of the text of the measure; and

   (b)   a copy of the provisions of this Act and the regulations that relate to the measure.

Giving notice to flag State for boat

(3)   When, or as soon as practicable after, an officer first exercises a power on the boat, an officer must give notice to the country of nationality that an officer has boarded and is inspecting the boat.

Leaving quickly after finding no evidence

(4)   The officer must leave the boat as soon as reasonably practicable after exercising the powers on the boat and finding no evidence that a person has seriously violated an Australian regional management measure in relation to the boat.

Giving report of exercise of powers

(5)   After one or more officers have finished exercising powers on the boat, an officer must give the master and the country of nationality of the boat a report of the exercise of the powers on the boat during the period while one or more officers were on the boat.

Report to note master's statements

(6)   The report must include a note of any objection or statement the master of the boat asked an officer to include in the report.

. . .

Officers to comply with regulations

(8)   The officer must comply with any other requirements prescribed by the regulations in relation to the exercise of the powers.

In addition, section 87G provides for a full set of officers' powers to apply to Australian-flagged boats when they are outside the AFZ. This in effect enables Australia to fulfill its responsibilities as a flag state in regard to Australian vessels wherever its vessels are.[105]

When a boat is suspected to be without nationality, the act makes the following provision in its section 87H:[106]

87H Officers' powers: boat on high seas without nationality
Power to board and inspect

(1)   An officer may board and inspect a boat on the high seas that is equipped for fishing if the officer has reasonable grounds to believe that the boat does not have a nationality.
       Note: If the officer discovers after boarding that the boat is in fact an FSA boat or an Australian-flagged boat, section 87B or 87G will apply section 84 to allow the officer to exercise powers on the boat.

Producing identification for master to inspect

(2)   The officer must produce written identification of the officer for the master of the boat to inspect as soon as practicable after the officer has boarded. If the officer does not do so, he or she must not remain on the boat.

Giving report of exercise of powers

(3)   After one or more officers have finished inspecting the boat, an officer must give the master of the boat a report of the inspection during the period while one or more officers were on the boat.

Report to note master's statements

(4)   The report must include a note of any objection or statement the master of the boat asked an officer to include in the report.

Minimising duplication

(5) This section does not require:

    (a) more than one report to be given in relation to the period for which one or more officers are on the boat (even if the same officer is not on the boat throughout the period); or

    (b) a report to be given to the master if section 87F requires a report to be given to the master.

    Note: Section 87F will require a report to be given to the master if the boat is in fact an FSA boat (despite there having been reasonable grounds to believe it was without nationality).

Several other provisions have been added to the act in order to bring it into line with the 1995 agreement, including for example, the provision for the handing over to its flag state of a boat that is believed to have committed a contravention on the high seas. Under the agreement, the flag state is able to take control and undertake its own investigation and enforcement action.[107]

The Australian legislation also introduces a new range of offenses. These are divided into two parts, the first concerning Australian-flagged boats beyond the AFZ, the second concerning FSA boats on the high seas. For the first category, a new offense is an Australian-flagged fishing boat taking or having possession of fish on the high seas without the necessary authorization (section 105A). Another section makes it an offense to have a boat without the necessary authorization. This provision merits being quoted in full as it is typical of the drafting adopted in Australia on such matters.

105B *Australian-flagged boat on high seas equipped for fishing*

(1) A person is guilty of an offence if:

    (a) a person intentionally has in his or her possession or charge an Australian-flagged boat; and

    (b) the boat is equipped with nets, traps or other equipment for fishing and the person is reckless as to that fact; and

    (c) the boat is at a place on the high seas and the person is reckless as to that fact.

(2) The offence is punishable on conviction by a fine of not more than 500 penalty units.

(3)   Subsection (1) does not apply if:

    (a)   the person holds a fishing concession or scientific permit authoris-ing the boat to be at that location equipped with nets, traps or other equipment for fishing; or

    (b)   the person is acting on behalf of the holder of such a concession or permit; or

    (c)   the boat is engaged solely in the ordinary course of trade of carrying cargo between:

        (i)   Australia and a foreign country; or

        (ii)   Australia and an external Territory; or

        (iii)   an external Territory and a foreign country; or

        (iv)   2 external Territories; or

    (d)   the person has a reasonable excuse.[108]

(4)   The only burden of proof that a defendant bears in respect of subsection (3) is the burden of adducing or pointing to evidence that suggests a reasonable possibility that the matter in question existed.

In this provision the offense is defined in very wide terms, which do not apply if certain conditions are established. The provision is also particularly interesting because it carefully addresses the question of proof. Basically the person will be found to have committed an offense on the basis of the easily met elements of subsection (1). This at first sight appears to reverse the burden of proof, but that particular problem is addressed in the final clause, by pointing out that the person charged has a limited burden to carry, namely that of "adducing or pointing to evidence that suggests a reasonable possibility that the matter in question existed." This is no doubt intended to avoid reversing the burden of proof in a more fundamental manner.[109]

Also within this new subsection is a provision that authorizes action by foreign officials against Australian-flagged boats, in essence giving effect to Article 21. This provision is also worth quoting in full:

105D *Authorising foreign officials' action affecting Australian-flagged boats*
Boarding boats suspected of illegal fishing in foreign waters

(1)   On behalf of Australia, AFMA may authorise officials of a foreign country that is party to the Fish Stocks Agreement to board and inspect an Aus-tralian-flagged boat on the high seas if:

(a) AFMA or Australia has received a request from the appropriate authority of the foreign country for that country's officials to board and inspect the boat; and

(b) AFMA has reasonable grounds to believe that the boat has been used for fishing in the exclusive economic zone, territorial sea, archipelagic waters (as defined in the United Nations Convention on the Law of the Sea) or internal waters of the foreign country without an authorisation (however described) given under the law of that country; and

(c) AFMA is satisfied that the boarding and inspection will be carried out in accordance with the Fish Stocks Agreement.

Investigating breach of regional management measures

(2) On behalf of Australia, AFMA may authorise an authority of a foreign country that is party to the Fish Stocks Agreement to investigate an alleged contravention of a regional management measure involving an Australian-flagged boat if:

(a) an official of the foreign country has boarded the boat on the high seas in an area covered by a regional organisation or arrangement; and

(b) the appropriate authority of the foreign country has notified AFMA or Australia that the official has reasonable grounds for believing that the boat has been used in contravention of the regional management measure; and

(c) AFMA is satisfied that the investigation will be carried out in accordance with the Fish Stocks Agreement.

Revocation of authorisation by AFMA

(3) AFMA may revoke an authorisation AFMA has given under this section.

Form of authorisation or revocation by AFMA

(4) An authorisation or revocation of an authorisation by AFMA must be in writing or by electronic transmission. However, an authorisation or revocation cannot be made by electronic transmission of an oral message.

Enforcement action for breach of regional management measures

(5) On behalf of Australia, the Attorney-General may authorise in writing an authority of a foreign country to take specified action to enforce a law of

the foreign country against a contravention of a regional management measure on the high seas involving an Australian-flagged boat if:

(a) AFMA has authorised an authority of the foreign country under subsection (2) to investigate the alleged contravention; and

(b) the appropriate authority of the foreign country has communicated the results of the investigation to Australia; and

(c) the Attorney-General is satisfied that the action will be taken in accordance with the Fish Stocks Agreement.

Revocation of authorisation by Attorney-General

(6) The Attorney-General may revoke in writing an authorisation he or she has given under this section.

The provisions referred to above concerning the regulation of Australian-flagged boats have their full parallel with respect to Fish Stocks Agreement boats. To show the interrelation between these two sets of measures, it is probably worth again quoting the relevant provisions in full:

Subdivision B—FSA boats on high seas

105E *FSA boat contravening management measure on high seas*

(1) A person is guilty of an offence if:

(a) the person intentionally uses an FSA boat; and

(b) the person intentionally contravenes an Australian regional management measure relating to the use of the boat; and

(c) the boat is on the high seas in an area covered by the regional organisation or arrangement that established the measure, and the person is reckless as to that fact.

. . .

105F *FSA boat fishing on high seas without flag state's authority*

(1) A person is guilty of an offence if:

(a) the person intentionally uses an FSA boat for fishing; and

(b) the boat is on the high seas in an area covered by a regional organisation or arrangement involving Australia, and the person is reckless as to that fact.

. . .

(3) Subsection (1) does not apply if the fishing is authorised by an authorisation (however described) issued under the law of the country of nationality of the FSA boat.

(4) The only burden of proof that a defendant bears in respect of subsection (3) is the burden of adducing or pointing to evidence that suggests a reasonable possibility that the matter in question existed.

The New Zealand and Australian laws also provide contrasting approaches to defining the term "serious violation" as that term is used in Article 21 of the Fish Stocks Agreement. The New Zealand Amendment of 1999 states simply: "'Serious violation' has the meaning given to it by Article 21.11 of the Fish Stocks Agreement." By contrast, the Australian amendment transforms the same definition into Australian law by the following provision:

(4) A person seriously violates an Australian regional management measure in relation to a boat if:

   (a) the person commits an offence against section 105E or 105F by:

   (i) using the boat to fish; or

   (ii) failing to maintain accurate records of fish taken using the boat; or

   (iii) failing to provide accurate information about fish taken, carried, transhipped or processed using the boat; or

   (iv) taking, carrying, transshipping or processing fish using the boat without an authorisation (however described) to do so; or

   (v) taking, carrying, transshipping or processing more fish using the boat than the person is authorised to do; or

   (vi) changing or hiding the markings of the boat; or

   (vii) a prescribed act or omission, or a prescribed series of acts or omissions, relating to the boat; or

   (b) the person conceals, tampers with or disposes of evidence of an offence against section 105E or 105F involving the boat; or

   (c) the person commits an offence relating to the boat against a prescribed provision of this Act or the regulations.

A further issue relates to the possible political sensitivity attached to such an action against a foreign vessel operating on the high seas. In common law jurisdictions the traditional way in which this is accommodated is to require the consent of the attorney general—the law officer of the government. This is done in the Australian legislation as follows:

105G *Attorney-General's consent required for prosecution*

(1) The Attorney-General's written consent is required before a charge of an offence against this Subdivision can proceed to hearing or determination.

(2) Before granting such a consent, the Attorney-General must take into account any views expressed by the government of the country of nationality of the FSA boat alleged to be involved in the offence.

(3) Even though the Attorney-General has not granted such a consent, the absence of consent is not to prevent or delay:

(a) the arrest of the suspected offender or proceedings related to arrest (such as proceedings for the issue and execution of a warrant); or

(b) the laying of a charge against the suspected offender; or

(c) proceedings for the extradition to Australia of the suspected offender; or

(d) proceedings for remanding the suspected offender in custody or on bail.

(4) If the Attorney-General declines to grant consent, the court in which the suspected offender has been charged with the offence must permanently stay proceedings on the charge.

(5) In any proceedings, an apparently genuine document purporting to be a copy of a written consent granted by the Attorney-General in accordance with this section will be accepted, in the absence of proof to the contrary, as proof of such consent.

Jurisdiction over "Nationals"

One issue that has been increasingly addressed in the context of the implementation of the Fish Stocks Agreement is the exercise of jurisdiction over "nationals," and the question is also being given extra attention in light of the recent FAO Initiative on Illegal, Unreported and Unregulated Fishing (IUU Fishing).[110] Before turning to the legislative provisions that deal with this, it is worth recalling briefly the international law background. The 1982

UN Convention, which permits states to draw on general international law,[111] gives exclusive jurisdiction over events on board a vessel on the high seas to the flag state.[112] One of the recognized bases of criminal jurisdiction in international law is jurisdiction based on the nationality of the perpetrator of a criminal act. This is often referred to as the "active nationality principle."

There is therefore no fundamental principle that would prevent a state from enacting a law that punishes its nationals for taking part in illegal fishing operations, or activities contrary to the FAO Compliance Agreement or the Fish Stocks Agreement—even if that national is on board a vessel flying the flag of another state. The main problem to which this gives rise, however, is a practical one: How does the state effectively enforce such a law? Not only may there be difficulties in obtaining custody of the alleged offender, but there may also be evidentiary problems if the evidence concerns events that occurred on board a foreign vessel.

This issue is of significance because of the language used in Articles 116, 117, 118, and 119(3) of the 1982 UN Convention. All these articles use the term "national" or "fisherman." This suggests that the term "nationals" takes its ordinary meaning of individuals of the relevant nationality. However, if one looks at the preceding 1958 Convention on Fishing and Conservation of the Living Resources of the High Seas, it is apparent that the term "nationals" is used in a different way. It is defined in Article 14 to retain what has been its traditional meaning as follows: "in Articles 1, 3, 4, 5, 6, and 8, the terms 'nationals' means fishing boats or craft of any size having the nationality of the state concerned, according to the law of that state, irrespective of the nationality of the members of their crews." However, this definition was dropped from the 1982 UN Convention. This omission has not to date been interpreted as giving rise to an exception to the exclusive jurisdiction of the flag state over a vessel on the high seas.

Nevertheless, given the obligations that the flag state has to require compliance with conservation and management measures relating to straddling fish stocks and highly migratory fish stocks on the high seas, jurisdiction over individuals is increasingly being regarded as one of the available "tools." There is, as indicated above, no reason in principle in general international law why states may not enact legislation to this effect.[113] A particularly strong instance of the exercise of this kind of jurisdiction is found in section 133E of the New Zealand legislation giving effect to the 1995 agreement, which, it will be recalled, is an amending act:

> No New Zealand national may use a vessel that is not registered under the Ship Registration Act 1992, or a tender of that vessel, to take (by any method) on the high seas any fish, aquatic life, or seaweed for sale, or to transport any fish, aquatic life, or seaweed taken on the high seas, except in accordance with an authorization issued by a state specified in subsection (2).

The authorizations referred to may be issued by a party to either the Fish Stocks Agreement or the Compliance Agreement, or by a state that is party to or has accepted the obligations of a global regional or subregional organization or arrangement to which the authorization relates. A particularly interesting provision relates further to an authorization by a state that "(i) is a signatory to the UN Fish Stocks Agreement; and (ii) has legislative and administrative mechanisms to control its vessels on the high seas in accordance with that agreement." Any person who contravenes this provision commits an offense and is liable to a penalty. Provision is made for a number of exemptions to be granted.[114] The importance of this provision is that it does not leave action solely to the flag state to control unauthorized fishing on the high seas. However, one important safeguard is written into this act, namely that the consent of the attorney general is required before proceedings can be instituted under these provisions.[115] This is a device that is intended to ensure that the primacy of the jurisdiction of the flag state is protected, as well as to provide a means of avoiding the risk of double jeopardy, jurisdictional conflicts, and other difficulties that might arise.

Interestingly, the IUU Fishing initiative has taken up this matter, and in the International Plan of Action (IPOA), it includes provisions calling for measures to be taken to exercise enforcement actions over "nationals," or more fully, "natural or legal persons" who may be subject to its jurisdiction including on the grounds of their nationality. Thus the IPOA text as agreed at the FAO Committee on Fisheries (COFI) reads:

> In the light of relevant provisions of the 1982 UN Convention, and without prejudice to the primary responsibility of the flag State on the high seas, each State should, to the greatest extent possible, take measures or cooperate to ensure that nationals subject to their jurisdiction do not support or engage in

IUU fishing. All States should cooperate to identify those nationals who are the operators or beneficial owners of vessels involved in IUU fishing.

States should discourage their nationals from flagging fishing vessels under the jurisdiction of a State that does not meet its flag State responsibilities.

What is interesting about these provisions is that in them, and elsewhere, the term "nationals" has been used with a deliberate ambiguity—for example, in paragraph 26. On the one hand, this was merely a call to use existing jurisdiction over nationals on the basis of the so-called active nationality principle of jurisdiction in international law. On the other hand, it was also intended to leave untouched the ambiguous reference in Articles 16–119 of the 1982 UN Convention about the use of that term.[116]

Port State Jurisdiction

One of the other developments that emerged in the IUU context—and that is relevant to both the Compliance Agreement and the Fish Stocks Agreement—is the attention being paid to port state controls.[117] This is dealt with here in relation to both instruments in view of the overlap between the two.

FAO Compliance Agreement

It will be recalled that the Compliance Agreement, in Article V (which is concerned with international cooperation), provides for port state control. When a fishing vessel is voluntarily in the port of a party other than its flag state, and when that party has reasonable grounds to believe that the fishing vessel has been used for an activity that undermines the effectiveness of international conservation and management measures, the party is to promptly notify the flag state. The provision also allows for arrangements to be made for port states to investigate to establish whether the fishing vessel has indeed been used in violation of the provisions of the agreement.

The U.S. High Seas Fishing Compliance Act puts this duty of international cooperation forward in a clear and detailed way in its section 105(c):

(c) *Information to Flag Nations—*
If the Secretary, in cooperation with the Secretary of State and the Secretary of the department in which the Coast Guard is operating, has reasonable

grounds to believe that a foreign vessel has engaged in activities undermining the effectiveness of international conservation and management measures, the Secretary shall—

(1) provide to the flag nation information, including appropriate evidentiary material, relating to those activities; and

(2) when such foreign vessel is voluntarily in a United States port, promptly notify the flag nation and, if requested by the flag nation, make arrangements to undertake such lawful investigatory measures as may be considered necessary to establish whether the vessel has been used contrary to the provisions of the Agreement.

It should be noted, however, that the requirement that the action be taken only at the request of the flag state is **not** required under the provisions of the Fish Stocks Agreement. This will be addressed later.

To implement Compliance Agreement requirements only, legislative provisions will still be needed to permit authorized officers to investigate foreign high seas vessels and enforce agreement measures when so requested by the flag state.

This appears in the OECS draft in the following way:

22. For the purpose of enforcing international conservation and management measures a national authorized officer may undertake inspection measures in respect of a foreign fishing vessel which is voluntarily in a port or offshore terminal of (country).

23. For the purpose of enforcing international conservation and management measures, and with the written authorization of the Chief Fisheries Officer pursuant to the request of the flag State, a national authorized officer may undertake specified enforcement measures in respect of a foreign fishing vessel which is voluntarily in a port or offshore terminal of (country).

Fish Stocks Agreement

In contrast with Article V of the Compliance Agreement—which, as we have seen, imposes a specific obligation to notify the flag state and request its agreement before port state investigatory and enforcement measures can be taken—the Fish Stocks Agreement, Article 23, imposes a more general duty:

A port State has the right and the duty to take measures, in accordance with international law, to promote the effectiveness of subregional, regional and global conservation and management measures.[118]

Article 23 further provides for inspection of documents, fishing gear, and catch on board fishing vessels, when such vessels are voluntarily in its ports or at its offshore terminals.[119] It also encourages states to "adopt regulations empowering the relevant national authorities to prohibit landings and transhipments where it has been established that the catch has been taken in a manner which undermines the effectiveness of subregional, regional or global conservation and management measures on the high seas."[120]

The New Zealand legislation has included a clause to provide for a measure of port state control. Section 113ZD provides:

(1) The master of a fishing vessel or fish carrier that is not a New Zealand ship, a New Zealand fishing vessel, or a registered fish carrier, who intends to bring the vessel into the internal waters of New Zealand, must give the chief executive at least 72 hours' notice, in the approved manner, of his or her intention to do so.

(2) If the chief executive is satisfied that a vessel has undermined international conservation and management measures, the chief executive may, by notice to the master of vessel to which subsection (1) applies, direct the vessel—

    (a) Not to enter the internal waters of New Zealand; or

    (b) If it has entered the internal waters, to leave those waters.

(3) If the Minister is satisfied on reasonable grounds that it is necessary for the purpose of the conservation and management of fish, aquatic life, or seaweed, the Minister may, by notice in the Gazette, direct any class or classes of fishing vessel or fish carrier not to enter the internal waters of New Zealand.

(4) The master of a vessel to which a notice under subsection (2) or (3) applies, who brings the vessel into the internal waters of New Zealand knowing that the vessel applies to the vessel, commits an offence and is liable to the penalty set out in section 252(5).

(5) This section does not prevent a vessel from entering or remaining in the internal waters of New Zealand for such period as is necessary for the

purposes of obtaining the food, fuel, and other goods and services necessary to enable the vessel to proceed safely and directly to a port outside New Zealand.[121]

In Australia, the 1991 Fisheries Management Act's section 102 had already provided the power to prohibit the entry into Australian ports of foreign fishing boats in certain circumstances. The same act also provided in section 103 that it was an offense for foreign boats to land fish in Australia in certain circumstances. This provision has now been replaced with a new one that is aimed at giving effect to Australia's obligations under the Fish Stocks Agreement. This provision reads:

(1)   A person is guilty of an offence if:
    (a)   the person is the master of a foreign boat; and
    (b)   the person intentionally lands or tranships (or causes to be landed or transhipped) fish from the boat at a place; and
    (c)   the place is in Australia or an external Territory and the person is reckless as to that fact.

   . . .

(1B) Subsection (1) does not apply if:
    (a)   the fish were landed or transhipped in accordance with:
       (i)   the terms of a foreign fishing licence; or
       (ii)   an entry under paragraph 21(2)(b) of the Torres Strait Fisheries Act 1984; or
       (iii) the terms of an approval given by the Minister; or
    (b)   the person has a reasonable excuse for causing the fish to be landed or transhipped.

(1C) The Minister may give a person written approval of the landing or transhipment of fish. The approval may be expressed to be subject to conditions.

(1D) The conditions to which an approval may be expressed to be subject include:
    (a)   a condition that the person (the approved person) to whom the approval relates notify a specified person of the landing or transhipment; and
    (b)   a condition that the approved person give a specified person a return of the species and quantity of fish landed or transhipped; and

(c) a condition that the landing or transhipment occur under the supervision of a specified person.

This does not limit subsection (1C).

(1E) The only burden of proof that a defendant bears in respect of subsection (1B) is the burden of adducing or pointing to evidence that suggests a reasonable possibility that the matter in question existed.

In the explanatory notes accompanying this amendment, its effect was described in the following terms:

The section provides for the regulation of foreign fishing boat landing and transshipment in port. Approval for landing and transshipment may be granted by the Minister and be subject to conditions. This regulation may be exercised to not permit landing of fish that is taken in a manner which either contravenes or undermines regional management arrangements for straddling or highly migratory fish stocks.

Norway also has the power to deny the use of port facilities in certain circumstances. In the "Regulations Relating to a Prohibition on Landing Fish Caught in Waters Outside Norwegian Jurisdiction," prohibitions are placed on the landing of certain catches. Thus in section 1 of the regulation,

It is prohibited to land catches of fish from fish stocks of mutual interest to Norway and other states which are not subject to agreed stock regulation measures or which are subject to Norwegian regulatory measures.

Likewise in section 2,

it is prohibited to land catches taken in contravention of a desired harvesting pattern or which may result in reasonable total quotas of the fish species in question being exceeded.

This is explained in the regulation as referring to catch from fish stocks that are subject to Norwegian regulatory measures and have not been taken pursuant to a fisheries agreement between Norway and the flag state, or by a vessel registered in a country with which Norway does not have a fisheries agreement.

Section 3 prohibits the landing of

catches consisting of fish caught in contravention of provisions laid down by regional or sub-regional fishery management organizations or arrangements, including catches taken by citizens of States that are not members of or parties to such organizations or arrangements.

These provisions are stated to apply irrespective of whether the fish have been caught in an area under the jurisdiction of a particular state or in international waters.[122]

In addition, there exists a more drastic power to deny access to vessels that have engaged in unregulated fishing on the high seas. This is described by Loebach in the following terms:

> Norwegian authorities have denied access to port by foreign fishing vessels that have taken part in an unregulated fishery on the high seas. A regulation concerning the entry into and passage through Norwegian territorial waters in peacetime of foreign non-military vessels stipulates that such vessels may be refused admission to Norwegian internal waters when special grounds make that necessary. [Amendment of 25 March 1994 of the regulation of 13 May 1977 relating to fishing and hunting operations by foreign nationals in the Exclusive Economic Zone of Norway.] Such special grounds exist, inter alia, when fishing vessels plan to enter these waters in connection with fishing, or bringing ashore a catch that implies that appropriate total quotas for the fish are being exceeded.[123]

Implementing Conservation and Management Measures

One matter that is common to both the Compliance Agreement and the Fish Stocks Agreement is the need to incorporate into national law certain conservation and management measures for the purpose of giving them domestic legal effect. This becomes extremely important in cases in which an element of an offense includes the violation of these measures. Indeed, a lack of certainty as to the conservation measure that is an element of a prosecution could well defeat it. In Namibia, in the Marine Resources Act, the following provision has been included in order to achieve this:

Giving effect to fisheries and international agreements

37. (1) The Minister may, for the purpose of any fisheries agreement entered into under section 35 or any international agreement to which

Namibia is a party, make such regulations as the Minister may consider necessary or expedient for the carrying out and for giving effect to the provisions of any such agreement or any amendment of such agreement.

(2) The Minister shall publish in the *Gazette* the texts of all conservation and management measures adopted under any international agreement to which Namibia is a party and any measure so published shall be deemed to be a regulation prescribed under section 61.

(3) For the purposes of—

   (a) subsection (2), "conservation and management measures" means measures to conserve and manage one or more species of living marine resources that are adopted and applied consistent with the relevant rules of international law as reflected in the United Nations Convention on the Law of the Sea of 10 December 1982, and the Implementation Agreement [i.e., the 1995 UN Fish Stocks Agreement].

Innovative Approaches

The Norwegian Regulations relating to fishing and hunting operations by foreign nationals in the economic zone of Norway

Norway has introduced regulations[124] that are at the forefront of attempts to control what is now coming to be known as illegal, unregulated, and unreported fishing. One regulation is aimed at controlling the activities of vessels fishing in the Barents Sea just outside the economic zone of Norway.

The critical provision reads:

Regulation 6:

   Even if other requirements are satisfied, the licence may be refused if, in areas under Norwegian fishery jurisdiction, the vessel's owner, master or crew have contravened the provisions relating to fishing and hunting operations or the conditions prescribed in a licence granted, or if the vessel has been used in connection with such a contravention. The same applies if the vessel or owner of the vessel has either taken part in fishing outside quota arrangements in international waters for a stock which is

> subject to regulation in waters under Norwegian fisheries jurisdiction or taken part in fishing operations that contravene regulatory measures laid down by regional or subregional fisheries management organizations or arrangements.

The effect of this provision is that a physical vessel may be denied a fishing license in Norwegian waters even if it is operated by persons other than those who participated in the fishing in that area just outside the economic zone.

"Long Arm" Jurisdiction

It is beyond the scope of this study to examine all the indirect means by which states can secure compliance with international obligations such as those contained in the Compliance Agreement and the Fish Stocks Agreement. One method, however, that has been adopted in a number of laws is the so-called "long arm" or Lacey Act laws. Such laws typically make it unlawful to import fish that have been taken in violation of the laws of another country.

In a study of national legislative options to combat IUU fishing, Kuemlangan gave, as a model of such a provision, the following:

(1) Subject to subsection (3), a person who, in (insert name of country) or in fisheries waters—

    (a) on his own account, or as partner, agent or employee of another person, lands, imports, exports, transports, sells, receives, acquires or purchases; or

    (b) causes or permits a person acting on his behalf, or uses a fishing vessel, to land, import, export, transport, sell, receive, acquire or purchase, any fish taken, possessed, transported or sold contrary to the law of another State shall be guilty of an offence and shall be liable to a fine not exceeding (insert monetary value).

(2) This section does not apply to fish taken on the high seas contrary to the laws of another State where (insert name of country) does not recognise the right of that State to make laws in respect of those fish.

(3) Where there is an agreement with another State relating to an offence referred to in subsection (1) (b), the penalty provided by subsection (1), or any portion of it according to the terms of the agreement, shall, after all

the costs and expenses have been deducted, be remitted to that State according to the terms of the agreement.[125]

Provision of Data

Most fisheries laws already provide for the collection of information concerning catches and the like, which may be used as the basis for the formulation of conservation and management measures. The Fish Stocks Agreement has considerably strengthened the obligations of fishing states to collect and report data.[126]

Under the 1982 UN Convention, the collection of information and its exchange are referred to as an obligation;[127] however, the provisions themselves often seem to presume that a state undertaking fishing on the high seas has access to the necessary data in order to put in place meaningful conservation or management measures. The convention contains no specific or primary obligation to this effect. Since the coming into force of the 1982 Convention, however, it has come to be recognized that the whole issue of supply and collection of fisheries data needs to be addressed much more rigorously.

The Fish Stocks Agreement therefore reflects a much more elaborate and sophisticated approach to the collection of data. It imposes quite specific obligations on states. The system of collection and communication of data is so fundamental to effective conservation and management measures that many of the data provisions of the Fish Stocks Agreement could be put into effect at a national level even before the agreement comes into force. Indeed, this is already happening with the Compliance Agreement as a number of states are already providing the information they will be required to provide before the agreement comes into force. As it seems unlikely that a national statutory basis would be required for the provision of information, a similar approach could be taken with respect to the obligations under the Fish Stocks Agreement.

Duties to Collect and Share Fisheries Data

Article 5 is of direct relevance here. Its paragraph (j) provides that state parties "collect and share, in a timely manner, complete and accurate data concerning fishing activities on, inter alia, vessel position, catch of target and non-target species and fishing effort, as set out in Annex I, as well as information from national and international research programmes."

Article 6 (on the precautionary approach) makes reference to the need to collect data. Its paragraph 3(d) requires states to "develop data collection and research programmes to assess the impact of fishing on non-target and associated or dependent species and their environment. . . ."

The Fish Stocks Agreement also makes specific provision for flag state responsibility for provision of data. Article 14 reads:

> States shall ensure that fishing vessels flying their flag provide such information as may be necessary in order to fulfil their obligations under this Agreement. To this end, States shall in accordance with Annex I . . .

Article 14 then sets out the detailed conditions regarding the collection and exchange of scientific, technical, and statistical data.

This duty is reinforced by Article 18, which sets out the duties of the flag state, and which includes among the measures to be taken by the flag state in paragraph 3(e) "requirements for recording and timely reporting of vessel position, catch of target and non-target species, fishing effort and other relevant fisheries data in accordance with subregional, regional, and global standards for the collection of such data."

The obligations on flag states are complemented by Article 9 (on subregional and regional fisheries organizations and arrangements) and Article 10 (on the functions of subregional and regional fisheries management organizations and arrangements). The most important provisions for these purposes are in paragraphs (d), (e), and (f) of Article 10. These require that such organizations and arrangements must do the following:

(d) obtain and evaluate scientific advice, review the status of the stocks and assess the impact of fishing on non-target and associated or dependent species;

(e) agree on standards for collection, reporting, verification and exchange of data on fisheries for the stocks;

(f) compile and disseminate accurate and complete statistical data, as described in Annex I, to ensure that the best scientific evidence is available, while maintaining confidentiality where appropriate.

The most detailed provisions are found in Annex I, however. The general principles adumbrated in Article 1 of this annex start with the recognition that "the timely collection, compilation and analysis of data are fundamental to the effective conservation and management of straddling fish stocks and highly migratory fish stocks." The annex sets out elaborate provisions concerning data. It is important to note that the obligations are not simply placed on the flag state, but more generally on "states." Thus while the flag state has specific obligations (already set out in Articles 14 and 18 above), other states—for example, coastal states—also have responsibilities.

It is a basic premise that the primary obligation should be placed on the flag state of vessels that are engaged in fishing.[128] Article 5 requires vessels flying a state's flag to send to its national fisheries administration—and where agreed, to the relevant subregional or regional fisheries management organization or arrangement—log book data on catch and effort, including data on fishing operations on the high seas. In Article 7, on data exchange, flag states must share data with other flag states and relevant coastal states through appropriate subregional or regional fisheries management organizations or arrangements. Such organizations are also to compile these data and make them freely available in a timely manner and in an agreed-upon format to all interested states.

FINAL REMARKS

The purpose of this Guide has been to provide the parliamentary drafter or the legislator with an outline of some of the most significant provisions of the two agreements under review and a basic "tool kit" of approaches already adopted by other states in meeting the obligations of these agreements. The transformation of international law treaty obligations into national law is of course the exclusive preserve of the national system—provided always of course that the national legislation does actually fulfill those treaty obligations. It is therefore worth reiterating that the inclusion of the provisions of the legislation of any state in this Guide does not represent any form of endorsement by the authors of one approach over another; the national laws have been chosen to represent a variety of different approaches to the transformation of these new and complex treaty provisions into national law.

It is also worth mentioning in conclusion that these two innovative agreements, important as they are, will not by themselves solve the problem of providing a sound international legal framework for sustainable fisheries. Even when both these agreements are in force with a large number of state parties, there will still be many other ways in which law—at the national and international levels—can be used to strengthen still further the conservation and management of straddling and highly migratory fish stocks. Many new legal and practical techniques have also been discussed within the context of the FAO initiative on Illegal, Unreported and Unregulated Fishing (IUU Fishing), and in March 2001 the Committee on Fisheries of FAO approved an International Plan of Action on IUU Fishing, (subject to formal adoption by the FAO Council) which set out a suite of measures designed to tighten controls on fishing vessels seeking to avoid internationally agreed norms. Many of these measures depend on the national legislative frameworks developed in the two agreements discussed here.

APPENDIX I

Agreement to Promote Compliance with International Conservation and Management Measures by Fishing Vessels on the High Seas

PREAMBLE

The Parties to this Agreement,

Recognizing that all States have the right for their nationals to engage in fishing on the high seas, subject to the relevant rules of international law, as reflected in the United Nations Convention on the Law of the Sea,

Further recognizing that, under international law as reflected in the United Nations Convention on the Law of the Sea, all States have the duty to take, or to cooperate with other States in taking, such measures for their respective nationals as may be necessary for the conservation of the living resources of the high seas,

Acknowledging the right and interest of all States to develop their fishing sectors in accordance with their national policies, and the need to promote cooperation with developing countries to enhance their capabilities to fulfil their obligations under this Agreement,

Recalling that Agenda 21, adopted by the United Nations Conference on Environment and Development, calls upon States to take effective action, consistent with international law, to deter reflagging of vessels by their nationals as a means of avoiding compliance with applicable conservation and management rules for fishing activities on the high seas,

Further recalling that the Declaration of Cancun, adopted by the International Conference on Responsible Fishing, also calls on States to take action in this respect,

Bearing in mind that under Agenda 21, States commit themselves to the conservation and sustainable use of marine living resources on the high seas,

Calling upon States which do not participate in global, regional or subregional fisheries organizations or arrangements to join or, as appropriate, to enter into understandings with such organizations or with parties to such organizations or arrangements with a view to achieving compliance with international conservation and management measures,

Conscious of the duties of every State to exercise effectively its jurisdiction and control over vessels flying its flag, including fishing vessels and vessels engaged in the transshipment of fish,

Mindful that the practice of flagging or reflagging fishing vessels as a means of avoiding compliance with international conservation and management measures for living marine resources, and the failure of flag States to fulfil their responsibilities with respect to fishing vessels entitled to fly their flag, are among the factors that seriously undermine the effectiveness of such measures,

Realizing that the objective of this Agreement can be achieved through specifying flag States' responsibility in respect of fishing vessels entitled to fly their flags and operating on the high seas, including the authorization by the flag State of such operations, as well as through strengthened international cooperation and increased transparency through the exchange of information on high seas fishing,

Noting that this Agreement will form an integral part of the International Code of Conduct for Responsible Fishing called for in the Declaration of Cancun,

Desiring to conclude an international agreement within the framework of the Food and Agriculture Organization of the United Nations, hereinafter referred to as FAO, under Article XIV of the FAO Constitution,

Have agreed as follows:

ARTICLE I
Definitions

For the purposes of this Agreement:

    (a) "fishing vessel" means any vessel used or intended for use for the purposes of the commercial exploitation of living marine resources, including mother ships and any other vessels directly engaged in such fishing operations;

    (b) "international conservation and management measures" means measures to conserve or manage one or more species of living marine resources that are adopted and applied in accordance with the relevant rules of international law as reflected in the 1982 United Nations Convention on the Law of the Sea. Such measures may be adopted either by global, regional or subregional fisheries organizations, subject to the rights and obligations of their members, or by treaties or other international agreements;

  (c) "length" means

    (i) for any fishing vessel built after 18 July 1982, 96 percent of the total length on a waterline at 85 percent of the least moulded depth measured from the top of the keel, or the length from the foreside of the stem to the axis of the rudder stock on that waterline, if that be greater. In ships designed with a rake of keel the waterline on which this length is measured shall be parallel to the designed waterline;

    (ii) for any fishing vessel built before 18 July 1982, registered length as entered on the national register or other record of vessels;

  (d) "record of fishing vessels" means a record of fishing vessels in which are recorded pertinent details of the fishing vessel. It may constitute a separate record for fishing vessels or form part of a general record of vessels;

  (e) "regional economic integration organization" means a regional economic integration organization to which its Member States have transferred competence over matters covered by this Agreement, including the authority to make decisions binding on its Member States in respect of those matters;

  (f) "vessels entitled to fly its flag" and "vessels entitled to fly the flag of a State", includes vessels entitled to fly the flag of a Member State of a regional economic integration organization.

ARTICLE II
Application

1. Subject to the following paragraphs of this Article, this Agreement shall apply to all fishing vessels that are used or intended for fishing on the high seas.

2. A Party may exempt fishing vessels of less than 24 metres in length entitled to fly its flag from the application of this Agreement unless the

Party determines that such an exemption would undermine the object and purpose of this Agreement, provided that such exemptions:

(a) shall not be granted in respect of fishing vessels operating in fishing regions referred to in paragraph 3 below, other than fishing vessels that are entitled to fly the flag of a coastal State of that fishing region; and

(b) shall not apply to the obligations undertaken by a Party under paragraph 1 of Article III, or paragraph 7 of Article VI of this Agreement.

3. Without prejudice to the provisions of paragraph 2 above, in any fishing region where bordering coastal States have not yet declared exclusive economic zones, or equivalent zones of national jurisdiction over fisheries, such coastal States as are Parties to this Agreement may agree, either directly or through appropriate regional fisheries organizations, to establish a minimum length of fishing vessels below which this Agreement shall not apply in respect of fishing vessels flying the flag of any such coastal State and operating exclusively in such fishing region.

ARTICLE III
Flag State Responsibility

1. (a) Each Party shall take such measures as may be necessary to ensure that fishing vessels entitled to fly its flag do not engage in any activity that undermines the effectiveness of international conservation and management measures.

   (b) In the event that a Party has, pursuant to paragraph 2 of Article II, granted an exemption for fishing vessels of less than 24 metres in length entitled to fly its flag from the application of other provisions of this Agreement, such Party shall nevertheless take effective measures in respect of any such fishing vessel that undermines the effectiveness of international conservation and management measures. These measures shall be such as to ensure that the fishing vessel ceases to engage in activities that undermine the effectiveness of the international conservation and management measures.

2. In particular, no Party shall allow any fishing vessel entitled to fly its flag to be used for fishing on the high seas unless it has been authorized to be so used by the appropriate authority or authorities of that Party. A

fishing vessel so authorized shall fish in accordance with the conditions of the authorization.

3. No Party shall authorize any fishing vessel entitled to fly its flag to be used for fishing on the high seas unless the Party is satisfied that it is able, taking into account the links that exist between it and the fishing vessel concerned, to exercise effectively its responsibilities under this Agreement in respect of that fishing vessel.

4. Where a fishing vessel that has been authorized to be used for fishing on the high seas by a Party ceases to be entitled to fly the flag of that Party, the authorization to fish on the high seas shall be deemed to have been cancelled.

5. (a) No Party shall authorize any fishing vessel previously registered in the territory of another Party that has undermined the effectiveness of international conservation and management measures to be used for fishing on the high seas, unless it is satisfied that

    (i) any period of suspension by another Party of an authorization for such fishing vessel to be used for fishing on the high seas has expired; and

    (ii) no authorization for such fishing vessel to be used for fishing on the high seas has been withdrawn by another Party within the last three years.

    (b) The provisions of subparagraph (a) above shall also apply in respect of fishing vessels previously registered in the territory of a State which is not a Party to this Agreement, provided that sufficient information is available to the Party concerned on the circumstances in which the authorization to fish was suspended or withdrawn.

    (c) The provisions of subparagraphs (a) and (b) shall not apply where the ownership of the fishing vessel has subsequently changed, and the new owner has provided sufficient evidence demonstrating that the previous owner or operator has no further legal, beneficial or financial interest in, or control of, the fishing vessel.

    (d) Notwithstanding the provisions of subparagraphs (a) and (b) above, a Party may authorize a fishing vessel, to which those subparagraphs would otherwise apply, to be used for fishing on the high seas, where the Party concerned, after having taken into account all relevant facts, including the circumstances in which the fishing authorization has been withdrawn by the other Party or State, has determined that to grant an authorization to use the vessel for fishing on the high seas would not undermine the object and purpose of this Agreement.

6. Each Party shall ensure that all fishing vessels entitled to fly its flag that it has entered in the record maintained under Article IV are marked in such a way that they can be readily identified in accordance with generally accepted standards, such as the FAO Standard Specifications for the Marking and Identification of Fishing Vessels.

7. Each Party shall ensure that each fishing vessel entitled to fly its flag shall provide it with such information on its operations as may be necessary to enable the Party to fulfil its obligations under this Agreement, including in particular information pertaining to the area of its fishing operations and to its catches and landings.

8. Each Party shall take enforcement measures in respect of fishing vessels entitled to fly its flag which act in contravention of the provisions of this Agreement, including, where appropriate, making the contravention of such provisions an offence under national legislation. Sanctions applicable in respect of such contraventions shall be of sufficient gravity as to be effective in securing compliance with the requirements of this Agreement and to deprive offenders of the benefits accruing from their illegal activities. Such sanctions shall, for serious offences, include refusal, suspension or withdrawal of the authorization to fish on the high seas.

ARTICLE IV
Records of Fishing Vessels

Each Party shall, for the purposes of this Agreement, maintain a record of fishing vessels entitled to fly its flag and authorized to be used for fishing on the high seas, and shall take such measures as may be necessary to ensure that all such fishing vessels are entered in that record.

ARTICLE V
International Cooperation

1. The Parties shall cooperate as appropriate in the implementation of this Agreement, and shall, in particular, exchange information, including evidentiary material, relating to activities of fishing vessels in order to as-

sist the flag State in identifying those fishing vessels flying its flag reported to have engaged in activities undermining international conservation and management measures, so as to fulfil its obligations under Article III.

2. When a fishing vessel is voluntarily in the port of a Party other than its flag State, that Party, where it has reasonable grounds for believing that the fishing vessel has been used for an activity that undermines the effectiveness of international conservation and management measures, shall promptly notify the flag State accordingly. Parties may make arrangements regarding the undertaking by port States of such investigatory measures as may be considered necessary to establish whether the fishing vessel has indeed been used contrary to the provisions of this Agreement.

3. The Parties shall, when and as appropriate, enter into cooperative agreements or arrangements of mutual assistance on a global, regional, subregional or bilateral basis so as to promote the achievement of the objectives of this Agreement.

ARTICLE VI
Exchange of Information

1. Each Party shall make readily available to FAO the following information with respect to each fishing vessel entered in the record required to be maintained under Article IV:
   (a) name of fishing vessel, registration number, previous names (if known), and port of registry;
   (b) previous flag (if any);
   (c) International Radio Call Sign (if any);
   (d) name and address of owner or owners;
   (e) where and when built;
   (f) type of vessel;
   (g) length.

2. Each Party shall, to the extent practicable, make available to FAO the following additional information with respect to each fishing vessel entered in the record required to be maintained under Article IV:
   (a) name and address of operator (manager) or operators (managers) (if any);
   (b) type of fishing method or methods;

     (c) moulded depth;

     (d) beam;

     (e) gross register tonnage;

     (f) power of main engine or engines.

3.   Each Party shall promptly notify to FAO any modifications to the information listed in paragraphs 1 and 2 of this Article.

4.   FAO shall circulate periodically the information provided under paragraphs 1, 2, and 3 of this Article to all Parties, and, on request, individually to any Party. FAO shall also, subject to any restrictions imposed by the Party concerned regarding the distribution of information, provide such information on request individually to any global, regional or subregional fisheries organization.

5.   Each Party shall also promptly inform FAO of -

     (a) any additions to the record;

     (b) any deletions from the record by reason of -

        (i)   the voluntary relinquishment or nonrenewal of the fishing authorization by the fishing vessel owner or operator;

        (ii) the withdrawal of the fishing authorization issued in respect of the fishing vessel under paragraph 8 of Article III;

        (iii) the fact that the fishing vessel concerned is no longer entitled to fly its flag;

        (iv) the scrapping, decommissioning or loss of the fishing vessel concerned; or

        (v) any other reason.

6.   Where information is given to FAO under paragraph 5(b) above, the Party concerned shall specify which of the reasons listed in that paragraph is applicable.

7.   Each Party shall inform FAO of

     (a) any exemption it has granted under paragraph 2 of Article II, the number and type of fishing vessel involved and the geographical areas in which such fishing vessels operate; and

     (b) any agreement reached under paragraph 3 of Article II.

8.   (a) Each Party shall report promptly to FAO all relevant information regarding any activities of fishing vessels flying its flag that undermine the effectiveness of international conservation and management measures, including the identity of the fishing vessel or

vessels involved and measures imposed by the Party in respect of such activities. Reports on measures imposed by a Party may be subject to such limitations as may be required by national legislation with respect to confidentiality, including, in particular, confidentiality regarding measures that are not yet final.

(b) Each Party, where it has reasonable grounds to believe that a fishing vessel not entitled to fly its flag has engaged in any activity that undermines the effectiveness of international conservation and management measures, shall draw this to the attention of the flag State concerned and may, as appropriate, draw it to the attention of FAO. It shall provide the flag State with full supporting evidence and may provide FAO with a summary of such evidence. FAO shall not circulate such information until such time as the flag State has had an opportunity to comment on the allegation and evidence submitted, or to object as the case may be.

9. Each Party shall inform FAO of any cases where the Party, pursuant to paragraph 5(d) of Article III, has granted an authorization notwithstanding the provisions of paragraph 5(a) or 5(b) of Article III. The information shall include pertinent data permitting the identification of the fishing vessel and the owner or operator and, as appropriate, any other information relevant to the Party's decision.

10. FAO shall circulate promptly the information provided under paragraphs 5, 6, 7, 8 and 9 of this Article to all Parties, and, on request, individually to any Party. FAO shall also, subject to any restrictions imposed by the Party concerned regarding the distribution of information, provide such information promptly on request individually to any global, regional or subregional fisheries organization.

11. The Parties shall exchange information relating to the implementation of this Agreement, including through FAO and other appropriate global, regional and subregional fisheries organizations.

ARTICLE VII
Cooperation with Developing Countries

The Parties shall cooperate, at a global, regional, subregional or bilateral level, and, as appropriate, with the support of FAO and other international or regional organizations, to provide assistance, including technical assistance, to Parties that are developing countries in order to assist them in fulfilling their obligations under this Agreement.

ARTICLE VIII
NonParties

1.   The Parties shall encourage any State not party to this Agreement to accept this Agreement and shall encourage any nonParty to adopt laws and regulations consistent with the provisions of this Agreement.
2.   The Parties shall cooperate in a manner consistent with this Agreement and with international law to the end that fishing vessels entitled to fly the flags of nonParties do not engage in activities that undermine the effectiveness of international conservation and management measures.
3.   The Parties shall exchange information amongst themselves, either directly or through FAO, with respect to activities of fishing vessels flying the flags of nonParties that undermine the effectiveness of international conservation and management measures.

ARTICLE IX
Settlement of Disputes

1.   Any Party may seek consultations with any other Party or Parties on any dispute with regard to the interpretation or application of the provisions of this Agreement with a view to reaching a mutually satisfactory solution as soon as possible.
2.   In the event that the dispute is not resolved through these consultations within a reasonable period of time, the Parties in question shall consult among themselves as soon as possible with a view to having the dispute settled by negotiation, inquiry, mediation, conciliation, arbitration, judicial settlement or other peaceful means of their own choice.
3.   Any dispute of this character not so resolved shall, with the consent of all Parties to the dispute, be referred for settlement to the International Court of Justice, to the International Tribunal for the Law of the Sea upon entry into force of the 1982 United Nations Convention on the Law of the Sea or to arbitration. In the case of failure to reach agreement on referral to the International Court of Justice, to the International Tri-

bunal for the Law of the Sea or to arbitration, the Parties shall continue to consult and cooperate with a view to reaching settlement of the dispute in accordance with the rules of international law relating to the conservation of living marine resources.

ARTICLE X
Acceptance

1. This Agreement shall be open to acceptance by any Member or Associate Member of FAO, and to any nonmember State that is a Member of the United Nations, or of any of the specialized agencies of the United Nations or of the International Atomic Energy Agency.
2. Acceptance of this Agreement shall be effected by the deposit of an instrument of acceptance with the Director-General of FAO, hereinafter referred to as the Director-General.
3. The Director-General shall inform all Parties, all Members and Associate Members of FAO and the SecretaryGeneral of the United Nations of all instruments of acceptance received.
4. When a regional economic integration organization becomes a Party to this Agreement, such regional economic integration organization shall, in accordance with the provisions of Article II.7 of the FAO Constitution, as appropriate, notify such modifications or clarifications to its declaration of competence submitted under Article II.5 of the FAO Constitution as may be necessary in light of its acceptance of this Agreement. Any Party to this Agreement may, at any time, request a regional economic integration organization that is a Party to this Agreement to provide information as to which, as between the regional economic integration organization and its Member States, is responsible for the implementation of any particular matter covered by this Agreement. The regional economic integration organization shall provide this information within a reasonable time.

ARTICLE XI
Entry into Force

1. This Agreement shall enter into force as from the date of receipt by the Director-General of the twenty-fifth instrument of acceptance.

2. For the purpose of this Article, an instrument deposited by a regional economic integration organization shall not be counted as additional to those deposited by Member States of such an organization.

ARTICLE XII
Reservations

Acceptance of this Agreement may be made subject to reservations which shall become effective only upon unanimous acceptance by all Parties to this Agreement. The Director-General shall notify forthwith all Parties of any reservation. Parties not having replied within three months from the date of the notification shall be deemed to have accepted the reservation. Failing such acceptance, the State or regional economic integration organization making the reservation shall not become a Party to this Agreement.

ARTICLE XIII
Amendments

1. Any proposal by a Party for the amendment of this Agreement shall be communicated to the Director-General.
2. Any proposed amendment of this Agreement received by the Director-General from a Party shall be presented to a regular or special session of the Conference for approval and, if the amendment involves important technical changes or imposes additional obligations on the Parties, it shall be considered by an advisory committee of specialists convened by FAO prior to the Conference.
3. Notice of any proposed amendment of this Agreement shall be transmitted to the Parties by the Director-General not later than the time when the agenda of the session of the Conference at which the matter is to be considered is dispatched.
4. Any such proposed amendment of this Agreement shall require the approval of the Conference and shall come into force as from the thirtieth day after acceptance by two-thirds of the Parties. Amendments involving new obligations for Parties, however, shall come into force in respect of each Party only on acceptance by it and as from the thirtieth day after such acceptance. Any amendment shall be deemed to involve new oblig-

ations for Parties unless the Conference. in approving the amendment, decides otherwise by consensus.

5. The instruments of acceptance of amendments involving new obligations shall be deposited with the Director-General, who shall inform all Parties of the receipt of acceptance and the entry into force of amendments.

6. For the purpose of this Article, an instrument deposited by a regional economic integration organization shall not be counted as additional to those deposited by Member States of such an organization.

ARTICLE XIV
Withdrawal

Any Party may withdraw from this Agreement at any time after the expiry of two years from the date upon which the Agreement entered into force with respect to that Party, by giving written notice of such withdrawal to the Director-General who shall immediately inform all the Parties and the Members and Associate Members of FAO of such withdrawal. Withdrawal shall become effective at the end of the calendar year following that in which the notice of withdrawal has been received by the Director-General.

ARTICLE XV
Duties of the Depositary

The Director-General shall be the Depositary of this Agreement. The Depositary shall:

(a) send certified copies of this Agreement to each Member and Associate Member of FAO and to such nonmember States as may become Party to this Agreement;

(b) arrange for the registration of this Agreement, upon its entry into force, with the Secretariat of the United Nations in accordance with Article 102 of the Charter of the United Nations;

(c) inform each Member and Associate Member of FAO and any nonmember States as may become Party to this Agreement of:

(i) instruments of acceptance deposited in accordance with Article X;

(ii) the date of entry into force of this Agreement in accordance with Article XI;

(iii) proposals for and the entry into force of amendments to this Agreement in accordance with Article XIII;

(iv) withdrawals from this Agreement pursuant to Article XIV.

ARTICLE XVI
Authentic Texts

The Arabic, Chinese, English, French, and Spanish texts of this Agreement are equally authentic.

APPENDIX II

Agreement for the Implementation of the Provisions of the United Nations Convention on the Law of the Sea of 10 December 1982 Relating to the Conservation and Management of Straddling Fish Stocks and Highly Migratory Fish Stocks

---

The States Parties to this Agreement,

Recalling the relevant provisions of the United Nations Convention on the Law of the Sea of 10 December 1982,

Determined to ensure the long-term conservation and sustainable use of straddling fish stocks and highly migratory fish stocks,

Resolved to improve cooperation between States to that end,

Calling for more effective enforcement by flag States, port States and coastal States of the conservation and management measures adopted for such stocks,

Seeking to address in particular the problems identified in chapter 17, programme area C, of Agenda 21 adopted by the United Nations Conference on Environment and Development, namely, that the management of high seas fisheries is inadequate in many areas and that some resources are overutilized; noting that there are problems of unregulated fishing, over-capitalization, excessive fleet size, vessel reflagging to escape controls, insufficiently selective gear, unreliable databases and lack of sufficient cooperation between States,

Committing themselves to responsible fisheries,

Conscious of the need to avoid adverse impacts on the marine environment, preserve biodiversity, maintain the integrity of marine ecosystems and minimize the risk of long-term or irreversible effects of fishing operations,

Recognizing the need for specific assistance, including financial, scientific and technological assistance, in order that developing States can participate effectively in the conservation, management and sustainable use of straddling fish stocks and highly migratory fish stocks,

Convinced that an agreement for the implementation of the relevant provisions of the Convention would best serve these purposes and contribute to
the maintenance of international peace and security,

Affirming that matters not regulated by the Convention or by this Agreement continue to be governed by the rules and principles of general international law,

Have agreed as follows:

Part I
General Provisions

Article 1
Use of terms and scope

1. For the purposes of this Agreement:
    (a) "Convention" means the United Nations Convention on the Law of
        the Sea of 10 December 1982;
    (b) "conservation and management measures" means measures to con-
        serve and manage one or more species of living marine resources
        that are adopted and applied consistent with the relevant rules of in-
        ternational law as reflected in the Convention and this Agreement;
    (c) "fish" includes molluscs and crustaceans except those belonging to
        sedentary species as defined in article 77 of the Convention; and
    (d) "arrangement" means a cooperative mechanism established in ac-
        cordance with the Convention and this Agreement by two or more
        States for the purpose, inter alia, of establishing conservation and
        management measures in a subregion or region for one or more
        straddling fish stocks or highly migratory fish stocks.
2. (a) "States Parties" means States which have consented to be bound by
        this Agreement and for which the Agreement is in force.
    (b) This Agreement applies mutatis mutandis:
        (i) to any entity referred to in article 305, paragraph 1 (c), (d) and
             (e), of the Convention and
        (ii) subject to article 47, to any entity referred to as an "internation-
             al organization" in Annex IX, article 1, of the Convention
             which becomes a Party to this Agreement, and to that extent
             "States Parties" refers to those entities.

3. This Agreement applies mutatis mutandis to other fishing entities whose vessels fish on the high seas.

Article 2
Objective

The objective of this Agreement is to ensure the long-term conservation and sustainable use of straddling fish stocks and highly migratory fish stocks through effective implementation of the relevant provisions of the Convention.

Article 3
Application

1. Unless otherwise provided, this Agreement applies to the conservation and management of straddling fish stocks and highly migratory fish stocks beyond areas under national jurisdiction, except that articles 6 and 7 apply also to the conservation and management of such stocks within areas under national jurisdiction, subject to the different legal regimes that apply within areas under national jurisdiction and in areas beyond national jurisdiction as provided for in the Convention.
2. In the exercise of its sovereign rights for the purpose of exploring and exploiting, conserving and managing straddling fish stocks and highly migratory fish stocks within areas under national jurisdiction, the coastal State shall apply mutatis mutandis the general principles enumerated in article 5.
3. States shall give due consideration to the respective capacities of developing States to apply articles 5, 6 and 7 within areas under national jurisdiction and their need for assistance as provided for in this Agreement. To this end, Part VII applies mutatis mutandis in respect of areas under national jurisdiction.

Article 4
Relationship between this Agreement and the Convention

Nothing in this Agreement shall prejudice the rights, jurisdiction and duties of States under the Convention. This Agreement shall be interpreted and applied in the context of and in a manner consistent with the Convention.

Part II
Conservation and Management of Straddling Fish Stocks
and Highly Migratory Fish Stocks

Article 5
General principles

In order to conserve and manage straddling fish stocks and highly migratory fish stocks, coastal States and States fishing on the high seas shall, in giving effect to their duty to cooperate in accordance with the Convention:

(a)   adopt measures to ensure long-term sustainability of straddling fish stocks and highly migratory fish stocks and promote the objective of their optimum utilization;

(b)   ensure that such measures are based on the best scientific evidence available and are designed to maintain or restore stocks at levels capable of producing maximum sustainable yield, as qualified by relevant environmental and economic factors, including the special requirements of developing States, and taking into account fishing patterns, the interdependence of stocks and any generally recommended international minimum standards, whether subregional, regional or global;

(c)   apply the precautionary approach in accordance with article 6;

(d)   assess the impacts of fishing, other human activities and environmental factors on target stocks and species belonging to the same ecosystem or associated with or dependent upon the target stocks;

(e)   adopt, where necessary, conservation and management measures for species belonging to the same ecosystem or associated with or dependent upon the target stocks, with a view to maintaining or restoring populations of such species above levels at which their reproduction may become seriously threatened;

(f)   minimize pollution, waste, discards, catch by lost or abandoned gear, catch of non-target species, both fish and non-fish species, (hereinafter referred to as non-target species) and impacts on associated or dependent species, in particular endangered species, through measures including, to the extent practicable, the development and use of selective, environmentally safe and cost-effective fishing gear and techniques;

   (g) protect biodiversity in the marine environment;

   (h) take measures to prevent or eliminate overfishing and excess fishing capacity and to ensure that levels of fishing effort do not exceed those commensurate with the sustainable use of fishery resources;

   (i) take into account the interests of artisanal and subsistence fishers;

   (j) collect and share, in a timely manner, complete and accurate data concerning fishing activities on, inter alia, vessel position, catch of target and non-target species and fishing effort, as set out in Annex I, as well as information from national and international research programmes;

   (k) promote and conduct scientific research and develop appropriate technologies in support of fishery conservation and management; and

   (l) implement and enforce conservation and management measures through effective monitoring, control and surveillance.

Article 6
Application of the precautionary approach

1.   States shall apply the precautionary approach widely to conservation, management and exploitation of straddling fish stocks and highly migratory fish stocks in order to protect the living marine resources and preserve the marine environment.

2.   States shall be more cautious when information is uncertain, unreliable or inadequate. The absence of adequate scientific information shall not be used as a reason for postponing or failing to take conservation and management measures.

3.   In implementing the precautionary approach, States shall:

   (a) improve decision-making for fishery resource conservation and management by obtaining and sharing the best scientific information available and implementing improved techniques for dealing with risk and uncertainty;

   (b) apply the guidelines set out in Annex II and determine, on the basis of the best scientific information available, stock-specific reference points and the action to be taken if they are exceeded;

(c) take into account, inter alia, uncertainties relating to the size and productivity of the stocks, reference points, stock condition in relation to such reference points, levels and distribution of fishing mortality and the impact of fishing activities on non-target and associated or dependent species, as well as existing and predicted oceanic, environmental and socio-economic conditions; and

(d) develop data collection and research programmes to assess the impact of fishing on non-target and associated or dependent species and their environment, and adopt plans which are necessary to ensure the conservation of such species and to protect habitats of special concern.

4. States shall take measures to ensure that, when reference points are approached, they will not be exceeded. In the event that they are exceeded, States shall, without delay, take the action determined under paragraph 3 (b) to restore the stocks.

5. Where the status of target stocks or non-target or associated or dependent species is of concern, States shall subject such stocks and species to enhanced monitoring in order to review their status and the efficacy of conservation and management measures. They shall revise those measures regularly in the light of new information.

6. For new or exploratory fisheries, States shall adopt as soon as possible cautious conservation and management measures, including, inter alia, catch limits and effort limits. Such measures shall remain in force until there are sufficient data to allow assessment of the impact of the fisheries on the long-term sustainability of the stocks, whereupon conservation and management measures based on that assessment shall be implemented. The latter measures shall, if appropriate, allow for the gradual development of the fisheries.

7. If a natural phenomenon has a significant adverse impact on the status of straddling fish stocks or highly migratory fish stocks, States shall adopt conservation and management measures on an emergency basis to ensure that fishing activity does not exacerbate such adverse impact. States shall also adopt such measures on an emergency basis where fishing activity presents a serious threat to the sustainability of such stocks. Measures taken on an emergency basis shall be temporary and shall be based on the best scientific evidence available.

Article 7
Compatibility of conservation and management measures

1. Without prejudice to the sovereign rights of coastal States for the pur-
    pose of exploring and exploiting, conserving and managing the liv-
    ing marine resources within areas under national jurisdiction as pro-
    vided for in the Convention, and the right of all States for their
    nationals to engage in fishing on the high seas in accordance with
    the Convention:

    (a) with respect to straddling fish stocks, the relevant coastal States and
         the States whose nationals fish for such stocks in the adjacent high
         seas area shall seek, either directly or through the appropriate mech-
         anisms for cooperation provided for in Part III, to agree upon the
         measures necessary for the conservation of these stocks in the adja-
         cent high seas area;

    (b) with respect to highly migratory fish stocks, the relevant coastal
         States and other States whose nationals fish for such stocks in the re-
         gion shall cooperate, either directly or through the appropriate
         mechanisms for cooperation provided for in Part III, with a view to
         ensuring conservation and promoting the objective of optimum uti-
         lization of such stocks throughout the region, both within and be-
         yond the areas under national jurisdiction.

2. Conservation and management measures established for the high seas
    and those adopted for areas under national jurisdiction shall be compati-
    ble in order to ensure conservation and management of the straddling
    fish stocks and highly migratory fish stocks in their entirety. To this end,
    coastal States and States fishing on the high seas have a duty to cooper-
    ate for the purpose of achieving compatible measures in respect of such
    stocks. In determining compatible conservation and management mea-
    sures, States shall:

    (a) take into account the conservation and management measures
         adopted and applied in accordance with article 61 of the Conven-
         tion in respect of the same stocks by coastal States within areas un-
         der national jurisdiction and ensure that measures established in re-
         spect of such stocks for the high seas do not undermine the
         effectiveness of such measures;

    (b) take into account previously agreed measures established and applied for the high seas in accordance with the Convention in respect of the same stocks by relevant coastal States and States fishing on the high seas;

    (c) take into account previously agreed measures established and applied in accordance with the Convention in respect of the same stocks by a subregional or regional fisheries management organization or arrangement;

    (d) take into account the biological unity and other biological characteristics of the stocks and the relationships between the distribution of the stocks, the fisheries and the geographical particularities of the region concerned, including the extent to which the stocks occur and are fished in areas under national jurisdiction;

    (e) take into account the respective dependence of the coastal States and the States fishing on the high seas on the stocks concerned; and

    (f) ensure that such measures do not result in harmful impact on the living marine resources as a whole.

3.   In giving effect to their duty to cooperate, States shall make every effort to agree on compatible conservation and management measures within a reasonable period of time.

4.   If no agreement can be reached within a reasonable period of time, any of the States concerned may invoke the procedures for the settlement of disputes provided for in Part VIII.

5.   Pending agreement on compatible conservation and management measures, the States concerned, in a spirit of understanding and cooperation, shall make every effort to enter into provisional arrangements of a practical nature. In the event that they are unable to agree on such arrangements, any of the States concerned may, for the purpose of obtaining provisional measures, submit the dispute to a court or tribunal in accordance with the procedures for the settlement of disputes provided for in Part VIII.

6.   Provisional arrangements or measures entered into or prescribed pursuant to paragraph 5 shall take into account the provisions of this Part, shall have due regard to the rights and obligations of all States concerned, shall not jeopardize or hamper the reaching of final agreement on compatible conservation and management measures and

shall be without prejudice to the final outcome of any dispute settlement procedure.

7. Coastal States shall regularly inform States fishing on the high seas in the subregion or region, either directly or through appropriate subregional or regional fisheries management organizations or arrangements, or through other appropriate means, of the measures they have adopted for straddling fish stocks and highly migratory fish stocks within areas under their national jurisdiction.

8. States fishing on the high seas shall regularly inform other interested States, either directly or through appropriate subregional or regional fisheries management organizations or arrangements, or through other appropriate means, of the measures they have adopted for regulating the activities of vessels flying their flag which fish for such stocks on the high seas.

Part III

Mechanisms for International Cooperation Concerning Straddling Fish Stocks and Highly Migratory Fish Stocks

Article 8
Cooperation for conservation and management

1. Coastal States and States fishing on the high seas shall, in accordance with the Convention, pursue cooperation in relation to straddling fish stocks and highly migratory fish stocks either directly or through appropriate subregional or regional fisheries management organizations or arrangements, taking into account the specific characteristics of the subregion or region, to ensure effective conservation and management of such stocks.

2. States shall enter into consultations in good faith and without delay, particularly where there is evidence that the straddling fish stocks and highly migratory fish stocks concerned may be under threat of over-exploitation or where a new fishery is being developed for such stocks. To this end, consultations may be initiated at the request of any interested State with a view to establishing appropriate arrangements to ensure conservation and management of the stocks. Pending agreement on such arrangements, States shall observe the provisions of this Agreement and

shall act in good faith and with due regard to the rights, interests and duties of other States.

3. Where a subregional or regional fisheries management organization or arrangement has the competence to establish conservation and management measures for particular straddling fish stocks or highly migratory fish stocks, States fishing for the stocks on the high seas and relevant coastal States shall give effect to their duty to cooperate by becoming members of such organization or participants in such arrangement, or by agreeing to apply the conservation and management measures established by such organization or arrangement. States having a real interest in the fisheries concerned may become members of such organization or participants in such arrangement. The terms of participation in such organization or arrangement shall not preclude such States from membership or participation; nor shall they be applied in a manner which discriminates against any State or group of States having a real interest in the fisheries concerned.

4. Only those States which are members of such an organization or participants in such an arrangement, or which agree to apply the conservation and management measures established by such organization or arrangement, shall have access to the fishery resources to which those measures apply.

5. Where there is no subregional or regional fisheries management organization or arrangement to establish conservation and management measures for a particular straddling fish stock or highly migratory fish stock, relevant coastal States and States fishing on the high seas for such stock in the subregion or region shall cooperate to establish such an organization or enter into other appropriate arrangements to ensure conservation and management of such stock and shall participate in the work of the organization or arrangement.

6. Any State intending to propose that action be taken by an intergovernmental organization having competence with respect to living resources should, where such action would have a significant effect on conservation and management measures already established by a competent subregional or regional fisheries management organization or arrangement, consult through that organization or arrangement with its members or participants. To the extent practicable, such consultation should take

place prior to the submission of the proposal to the intergovernmental organization.

Article 9
Subregional and regional fisheries management organizations and arrangements

1. In establishing subregional or regional fisheries management organizations or in entering into subregional or regional fisheries management arrangements for straddling fish stocks and highly migratory fish stocks, States shall agree, inter alia, on:
    (a) the stocks to which conservation and management measures apply, taking into account the biological characteristics of the stocks concerned and the nature of the fisheries involved;
    (b) the area of application, taking into account article 7, paragraph 1, and the characteristics of the subregion or region, including socio-economic, geographical and environmental factors;
    (c) the relationship between the work of the new organization or arrangement and the role, objectives and operations of any relevant existing fisheries management organizations or arrangements; and
    (d) the mechanisms by which the organization or arrangement will obtain scientific advice and review the status of the stocks, including, where appropriate, the establishment of a scientific advisory body.
2. States cooperating in the formation of a subregional or regional fisheries management organization or arrangement shall inform other States which they are aware have a real interest in the work of the proposed organization or arrangement of such cooperation.

Article 10
Functions of subregional and regional fisheries management organizations
and arrangements

In fulfilling their obligation to cooperate through subregional or regional fisheries management organizations or arrangements, States shall:
    (a) agree on and comply with conservation and management measures to ensure the long-term sustainability of straddling fish stocks and highly migratory fish stocks;
    (b) agree, as appropriate, on participatory rights such as allocations of allowable catch or levels of fishing effort;

(c) adopt and apply any generally recommended international minimum standards for the responsible conduct of fishing operations;

(d) obtain and evaluate scientific advice, review the status of the stocks and assess the impact of fishing on non-target and associated or dependent species;

(e) agree on standards for collection, reporting, verification and exchange of data on fisheries for the stocks;

(f) compile and disseminate accurate and complete statistical data, as described in Annex I, to ensure that the best scientific evidence is available, while maintaining confidentiality where appropriate;

(g) promote and conduct scientific assessments of the stocks and relevant research and disseminate the results thereof;

(h) establish appropriate cooperative mechanisms for effective monitoring, control, surveillance and enforcement;

(i) agree on means by which the fishing interests of new members of the organization or new participants in the arrangement will be accommodated;

(j) agree on decision-making procedures which facilitate the adoption of conservation and management measures in a timely and effective manner;

(k) promote the peaceful settlement of disputes in accordance with Part VIII;

(l) ensure the full cooperation of their relevant national agencies and industries in implementing the recommendations and decisions of the organization or arrangement; and

(m) give due publicity to the conservation and management measures established by the organization or arrangement.

Article 11

New members or participants

In determining the nature and extent of participatory rights for new members of a subregional or regional fisheries management organization, or for new participants in a subregional or regional fisheries management arrangement, States shall take into account, inter alia:

(a) the status of the straddling fish stocks and highly migratory fish stocks and the existing level of fishing effort in the fishery;

(b) the respective interests, fishing patterns and fishing practices of new and existing members or participants;

(c) the respective contributions of new and existing members or participants to conservation and management of the stocks, to the collection and provision of accurate data and to the conduct of scientific research on the stocks;

(d) the needs of coastal fishing communities which are dependent mainly on fishing for the stocks;

(e) the needs of coastal States whose economies are overwhelmingly dependent on the exploitation of living marine resources; and

(f) the interests of developing States from the subregion or region in whose areas of national jurisdiction the stocks also occur.

Article 12
Transparency in activities of subregional and regional fisheries management organizations and arrangements

1. States shall provide for transparency in the decision-making process and other activities of subregional and regional fisheries management organizations and arrangements.

2. Representatives from other intergovernmental organizations and representatives from non-governmental organizations concerned with straddling fish stocks and highly migratory fish stocks shall be afforded the opportunity to take part in meetings of subregional and regional fisheries management organizations and arrangements as observers or otherwise, as appropriate, in accordance with the procedures of the organization or arrangement concerned. Such procedures shall not be unduly restrictive in this respect. Such intergovernmental organizations and non-governmental organizations shall have timely access to the records and reports of such organizations and arrangements, subject to the procedural rules on access to them.

Article 13
Strengthening of existing organizations and arrangements

States shall cooperate to strengthen existing subregional and regional fisheries management organizations and arrangements in order to improve their effectiveness in establishing and implementing conservation and management measures for straddling fish stocks and highly migratory fish stocks.

Article 14
Collection and provision of information and cooperation in scientific research

1. States shall ensure that fishing vessels flying their flag provide such information as may be necessary in order to fulfil their obligations under this Agreement. To this end, States shall in accordance with Annex I:

    (a) collect and exchange scientific, technical and statistical data with respect to fisheries for straddling fish stocks and highly migratory fish stocks;

    (b) ensure that data are collected in sufficient detail to facilitate effective stock assessment and are provided in a timely manner to fulfil the requirements of subregional or regional fisheries management organizations or arrangements; and

    (c) take appropriate measures to verify the accuracy of such data.

2. States shall cooperate, either directly or through subregional or regional fisheries management organizations or arrangements:

    (a) to agree on the specification of data and the format in which they are to be provided to such organizations or arrangements, taking into account the nature of the stocks and the fisheries for those stocks; and

    (b) to develop and share analytical techniques and stock assessment methodologies to improve measures for the conservation and management of straddling fish stocks and highly migratory fish stocks.

3. Consistent with Part XIII of the Convention, States shall cooperate, either directly or through competent international organizations, to strengthen scientific research capacity in the field of fisheries and promote scientific research related to the conservation and management of straddling fish stocks and highly migratory fish stocks for the benefit of all. To this end, a State or the competent international organization conducting such research beyond areas under national jurisdiction shall actively promote the publication and dissemination to any interested States of the results of that research and information relating to its objectives and methods and, to the extent practicable, shall facilitate the participation of scientists from those States in such research.

Article 15
Enclosed and semi-enclosed seas

In implementing this Agreement in an enclosed or semi-enclosed sea, States shall take into account the natural characteristics of that sea and shall also act in a manner consistent with Part IX of the Convention and other relevant provisions thereof.

Article 16
Areas of high seas surrounded entirely by an area under the national jurisdiction of a single State

1. States fishing for straddling fish stocks and highly migratory fish stocks in an area of the high seas surrounded entirely by an area under the national jurisdiction of a single State and the latter State shall cooperate to establish conservation and management measures in respect of those stocks in the high seas area. Having regard to the natural characteristics of the area, States shall pay special attention to the establishment of compatible conservation and management measures for such stocks pursuant to article 7. Measures taken in respect of the high seas shall take into account the rights, duties and interests of the coastal State under the Convention, shall be based on the best scientific evidence available and shall also take into account any conservation and management measures adopted and applied in respect of the same stocks in accordance with article 61 of the Convention by the coastal State in the area under national jurisdiction. States shall also agree on measures for monitoring, control, surveillance and enforcement to ensure compliance with the conservation and management measures in respect of the high seas.

2. Pursuant to article 8, States shall act in good faith and make every effort to agree without delay on conservation and management measures to be applied in the carrying out of fishing operations in the area referred to in paragraph 1. If, within a reasonable period of time, the fishing States concerned and the coastal State are unable to agree on such measures, they shall, having regard to paragraph 1, apply article 7, paragraphs 4, 5 and 6, relating to provisional arrangements or measures. Pending the establishment of such provisional arrangements or measures, the States concerned shall take measures in respect of vessels flying their flag in

order that they not engage in fisheries which could undermine the stocks concerned.

Part IV
Non-Members and Non-Participants

Article 17
Non-members of organizations and non-participant in arrangements

1   A State which is not a member of a subregional or regional fisheries management organization or is not a participant in a subregional or regional fisheries management arrangement, and which does not otherwise agree to apply the conservation and management measures established by such organization or arrangement, is not discharged from the obligation to cooperate, in accordance with the Convention and this Agreement, in the conservation and management of the relevant straddling fish stocks and highly migratory fish stocks.

2.   Such State shall not authorize vessels flying its flag to engage in fishing operations for the straddling fish stocks or highly migratory fish stocks which are subject to the conservation and management measures established by such organization or arrangement.

3.   States which are members of a subregional or regional fisheries management organization or participants in a subregional or regional fisheries management arrangement shall, individually or jointly, request the fishing entities referred to in article 1, paragraph 3, which have fishing vessels in the relevant area to cooperate fully with such organization or arrangement in implementing the conservation and management measures it has established, with a view to having such measures applied de facto as extensively as possible to fishing activities in the relevant area. Such fishing entities shall enjoy benefits from participation in the fishery commensurate with their commitment to comply with conservation and management measures in respect of the stocks.

4.   States which are members of such organization or participants in such arrangement shall exchange information with respect to the activities of fishing vessels flying the flags of States which are neither members of the organization nor participants in the arrangement and which are engaged in fishing operations for the relevant stocks. They shall take measures

consistent with this Agreement and international law to deter activities of such vessels which undermine the effectiveness of subregional or regional conservation and management measures.

Part V
Duties of the Flag State

Article 18
Duties of the flag State

1. A State whose vessels fish on the high seas shall take such measures as may be necessary to ensure that vessels flying its flag comply with subregional and regional conservation and management measures and that such vessels do not engage in any activity which undermines the effectiveness of such measures.
2. A State shall authorize the use of vessels flying its flag for fishing on the high seas only where it is able to exercise effectively its responsibilities in respect of such vessels under the Convention and this Agreement.
3. Measures to be taken by a State in respect of vessels flying its flag shall include:
   (a) control of such vessels on the high seas by means of fishing licences, authorizations or permits, in accordance with any applicable procedures agreed at the subregional, regional or global level;
   (b) establishment of regulations:
      (i) to apply terms and conditions to the licence, authorization or permit sufficient to fulfil any subregional, regional or global obligations of the flag State;
      (ii) to prohibit fishing on the high seas by vessels which are not duly licensed or authorized to fish, or fishing on the high seas by vessels otherwise than in accordance with the terms and conditions of a licence, authorization or permit;
      (iii) to require vessels fishing on the high seas to carry the licence, authorization or permit on board at all times and to produce it on demand for inspection by a duly authorized person; and
      (iv) to ensure that vessels flying its flag do not conduct unauthorized fishing within areas under the national jurisdiction of other States;

(c) establishment of a national record of fishing vessels authorized to fish on the high seas and provision of access to the information contained in that record on request by directly interested States, taking into account any national laws of the flag State regarding the release of such information;

(d) requirements for marking of fishing vessels and fishing gear for identification in accordance with uniform and internationally recognizable vessel and gear marking systems, such as the Food and Agriculture Organization of the United Nations Standard Specifications for the Marking and Identification of Fishing Vessels;

(e) requirements for recording and timely reporting of vessel position, catch of target and non-target species, fishing effort and other relevant fisheries data in accordance with subregional, regional and global standards for collection of such data;

(f) requirements for verifying the catch of target and non-target species through such means as observer programmes, inspection schemes, unloading reports, supervision of transshipment and monitoring of landed catches and market statistics;

(g) monitoring, control and surveillance of such vessels, their fishing operations and related activities by, inter alia:

(i) the implementation of national inspection schemes and subregional and regional schemes for cooperation in enforcement pursuant to articles 21 and 22, including requirements for such vessels to permit access by duly authorized inspectors from other States;

(ii) the implementation of national observer programmes and subregional and regional observer programmes in which the flag State is a participant, including requirements for such vessels to permit access by observers from other States to carry out the functions agreed under the programmes; and

(iii) the development and implementation of vessel monitoring systems, including, as appropriate, satellite transmitter systems, in accordance with any national programmes and those which have been subregionally, regionally or globally agreed among the States concerned;

(h) regulation of transshipment on the high seas to ensure that the effectiveness of conservation and management measures is not undermined; and

(i) regulation of fishing activities to ensure compliance with subregional, regional or global measures, including those aimed at minimizing catches of non-target species.

4. Where there is a subregionally, regionally or globally agreed system of monitoring, control and surveillance in effect, States shall ensure that the measures they impose on vessels flying their flag are compatible with that system.

Part VI
Compliance and Enforcement

Article 19
Compliance and enforcement by the flag State

1. A State shall ensure compliance by vessels flying its flag with subregional and regional conservation and management measures for straddling fish stocks and highly migratory fish stocks. To this end, that State shall:

(a) enforce such measures irrespective of where violations occur;

(b) investigate immediately and fully any alleged violation of subregional or regional conservation and management measures, which may include the physical inspection of the vessels concerned, and report promptly to the State alleging the violation and the relevant subregional or regional organization or arrangement on the progress and outcome of the investigation;

(c) require any vessel flying its flag to give information to the investigating authority regarding vessel position, catches, fishing gear, fishing operations and related activities in the area of an alleged violation;

(d) if satisfied that sufficient evidence is available in respect of an alleged violation, refer the case to its authorities with a view to instituting proceedings without delay in accordance with its laws and, where appropriate, detain the vessel concerned; and

(e) ensure that, where it has been established, in accordance with its laws, a vessel has been involved in the commission of a serious violation of such measures, the vessel does not engage in fishing operations on the high seas until such time as all outstanding sanctions imposed by the flag State in respect of the violation have been complied with.

2. All investigations and judicial proceedings shall be carried out expeditiously. Sanctions applicable in respect of violations shall be adequate in severity to be effective in securing compliance and to discourage violations wherever they occur and shall deprive offenders of the benefits accruing from their illegal activities. Measures applicable in respect of masters and other officers of fishing vessels shall include provisions which may permit, inter alia, refusal, withdrawal or suspension of authorizations to serve as masters or officers on such vessels.

Article 20
International cooperation in enforcement

1. States shall cooperate, either directly or through subregional or regional fisheries management organizations or arrangements, to ensure compliance with and enforcement of subregional and regional conservation and management measures for straddling fish stocks and highly migratory fish stocks.

2. A flag State conducting an investigation of an alleged violation of conservation and management measures for straddling fish stocks or highly migratory fish stocks may request the assistance of any other State whose cooperation may be useful in the conduct of that investigation. All States shall endeavour to meet reasonable requests made by a flag State in connection with such investigations.

3. A flag State may undertake such investigations directly, in cooperation with other interested States or through the relevant subregional or regional fisheries management organization or arrangement. Information on the progress and outcome of the investigations shall be provided to all States having an interest in, or affected by, the alleged violation.

4. States shall assist each other in identifying vessels reported to have engaged in activities undermining the effectiveness of subregional, regional or global conservation and management measures.

5. States shall, to the extent permitted by national laws and regulations, establish arrangements for making available to prosecuting authorities in other States evidence relating to alleged violations of such measures.

6. Where there are reasonable grounds for believing that a vessel on the high seas has been engaged in unauthorized fishing within an area under the jurisdiction of a coastal State, the flag State of that vessel, at the request of the coastal State concerned, shall immediately and fully investigate the matter. The flag State shall cooperate with the coastal State in taking appropriate enforcement action in such cases and may authorize the relevant authorities of the coastal State to board and inspect the vessel on the high seas. This paragraph is without prejudice to article 111 of the Convention.

7. States Parties which are members of a subregional or regional fisheries management organization or participants in a subregional or regional fisheries management arrangement may take action in accordance with international law, including through recourse to subregional or regional procedures established for this purpose, to deter vessels which have engaged in activities which undermine the effectiveness of or otherwise violate the conservation and management measures established by that organization or arrangement from fishing on the high seas in the subregion or region until such time as appropriate action is taken by the flag State.

Article 21
Subregional and regional cooperation in enforcement

1. In any high seas area covered by a subregional or regional fisheries management organization or arrangement, a State Party which is a member of such organization or a participant in such arrangement may, through its duly authorized inspectors, board and inspect, in accordance with paragraph 2, fishing vessels flying the flag of another State Party to this Agreement, whether or not such State Party is also a member of the organization or a participant in the arrangement, for the purpose of ensuring compliance with conservation and management measures for straddling fish stocks and highly migratory fish stocks established by that organization or arrangement.

2. States shall establish, through subregional or regional fisheries management organizations or arrangements, procedures for boarding and inspection pursuant to paragraph 1, as well as procedures to implement other provisions of this article. Such procedures shall be consistent with this article and the basic procedures set out in article 22 and shall not

discriminate against non-members of the organization or non-partici-pants in the arrangement. Boarding and inspection as well as any subse-quent enforcement action shall be conducted in accordance with such procedures. States shall give due publicity to procedures established pur-suant to this paragraph.

3. If, within two years of the adoption of this Agreement, any organization or arrangement has not established such procedures, boarding and in-spection pursuant to paragraph 1, as well as any subsequent enforce-ment action, shall, pending the establishment of such procedures, be conducted in accordance with this article and the basic procedures set out in article 22.

4. Prior to taking action under this article, inspecting States shall, either di-rectly or through the relevant subregional or regional fisheries manage-ment organization or arrangement, inform all States whose vessels fish on the high seas in the subregion or region of the form of identification issued to their duly authorized inspectors. The vessels used for boarding and inspection shall be clearly marked and identifiable as being on gov-ernment service. At the time of becoming a Party to this Agreement, a State shall designate an appropriate authority to receive notifications pursuant to this article and shall give due publicity of such designation through the relevant subregional or regional fisheries management orga-nization or arrangement.

5. Where, following a boarding and inspection, there are clear grounds for believing that a vessel has engaged in any activity contrary to the conser-vation and management measures referred to in paragraph 1, the in-specting State shall, where appropriate, secure evidence and shall promptly notify the flag State of the alleged violation.

6. The flag State shall respond to the notification referred to in paragraph 5 within three working days of its receipt, or such other period as may be prescribed in procedures established in accordance with paragraph 2, and shall either:

    (a) fulfil, without delay, its obligations under article 19 to investigate and, if evidence so warrants, take enforcement action with respect to the vessel, in which case it shall promptly inform the inspecting State of the results of the investigation and of any enforcement action taken; or

    (b) authorize the inspecting State to investigate.

7. Where the flag State authorizes the inspecting State to investigate an alleged violation, the inspecting State shall, without delay, communicate the results of that investigation to the flag State. The flag State shall, if evidence so warrants, fulfil its obligations to take enforcement action with respect to the vessel. Alternatively, the flag State may authorize the inspecting State to take such enforcement action as the flag State may specify with respect to the vessel, consistent with the rights and obligations of the flag State under this Agreement.

8. Where, following boarding and inspection, there are clear grounds for believing that a vessel has committed a serious violation, and the flag State has either failed to respond or failed to take action as required under paragraphs 6 or 7, the inspectors may remain on board and secure evidence and may require the master to assist in further investigation including, where appropriate, by bringing the vessel without delay to the nearest appropriate port, or to such other port as may be specified in procedures established in accordance with paragraph 2. The inspecting State shall immediately inform the flag State of the name of the port to which the vessel is to proceed. The inspecting State and the flag State and, as appropriate, the port State shall take all necessary steps to ensure the well-being of the crew regardless of their nationality.

9. The inspecting State shall inform the flag State and the relevant organization or the participants in the relevant arrangement of the results of any further investigation.

10. The inspecting State shall require its inspectors to observe generally accepted international regulations, procedures and practices relating to the safety of the vessel and the crew, minimize interference with fishing operations and, to the extent practicable, avoid action which would adversely affect the quality of the catch on board. The inspecting State shall ensure that boarding and inspection is not conducted in a manner that would constitute harassment of any fishing vessel.

11. For the purposes of this article, a serious violation means:
    (a) fishing without a valid licence, authorization or permit issued by the flag State in accordance with article 18, paragraph 3 (a);
    (b) failing to maintain accurate records of catch and catch-related data, as required by the relevant subregional or regional fisheries management organization or arrangement, or serious misreporting of

catch, contrary to the catch reporting requirements of such organization or arrangement;

(c) fishing in a closed area, fishing during a closed season or fishing without, or after attainment of, a quota established by the relevant subregional or regional fisheries management organization or arrangement;

(d) directed fishing for a stock which is subject to a moratorium or for which fishing is prohibited;

(e) using prohibited fishing gear;

(f) falsifying or concealing the markings, identity or registration of a fishing vessel;

(g) concealing, tampering with or disposing of evidence relating to an investigation;

(h) multiple violations which together constitute a serious disregard of conservation and management measures; or

(i) such other violations as may be specified in procedures established by the relevant subregional or regional fisheries management organization or arrangement.

12. Notwithstanding the other provisions of this article, the flag State may, at any time, take action to fulfil its obligations under article 19 with respect to an alleged violation. Where the vessel is under the direction of the inspecting State, the inspecting State shall, at the request of the flag State, release the vessel to the flag State along with full information on the progress and outcome of its investigation.

13. This article is without prejudice to the right of the flag State to take any measures, including proceedings to impose penalties, according to its laws.

14. This article applies mutatis mutandis to boarding and inspection by a State Party which is a member of a subregional or regional fisheries management organization or a participant in a subregional or regional fisheries management arrangement and which has clear grounds for believing that a fishing vessel flying the flag of another State Party has engaged in any activity contrary to relevant conservation and management measures referred to in paragraph 1 in the high seas area covered by such organization or arrangement, and such vessel has subsequently, during the same fishing trip, entered into an area under the national jurisdiction of the inspecting State.

15. Where a subregional or regional fisheries management organization or arrangement has established an alternative mechanism which effectively discharges the obligation under this Agreement of its members or participants to ensure compliance with the conservation and management measures established by the organization or arrangement, members of such organization or participants in such arrangement may agree to limit the application of paragraph 1 as between themselves in respect of the conservation and management measures which have been established in the relevant high seas area.

16. Action taken by States other than the flag State in respect of vessels having engaged in activities contrary to subregional or regional conservation and management measures shall be proportionate to the seriousness of the violation.

17. Where there are reasonable grounds for suspecting that a fishing vessel on the high seas is without nationality, a State may board and inspect the vessel. Where evidence so warrants, the State may take such action as may be appropriate in accordance with international law.

18. States shall be liable for damage or loss attributable to them arising from action taken pursuant to this article when such action is unlawful or exceeds that reasonably required in the light of available information to implement the provisions of this article.

Article 22
Basic procedures for boarding and inspection pursuant to article 21

1. The inspecting State shall ensure that its duly authorized inspectors:
   (a) present credentials to the master of the vessel and produce a copy of the text of the relevant conservation and management measures or rules and regulations in force in the high seas area in question pursuant to those measures;
   (b) initiate notice to the flag State at the time of the boarding and inspection;
   (c) do not interfere with the master's ability to communicate with the authorities of the flag State during the boarding and inspection;
   (d) provide a copy of a report on the boarding and inspection to the master and to the authorities of the flag State, noting therein any

objection or statement which the master wishes to have included in the report;

(e) promptly leave the vessel following completion of the inspection if they find no evidence of a serious violation; and

(f) avoid the use of force except when and to the degree necessary to ensure the safety of the inspectors and where the inspectors are obstructed in the execution of their duties. The degree of force used shall not exceed that reasonably required in the circumstances.

2. The duly authorized inspectors of an inspecting State shall have the authority to inspect the vessel, its licence, gear, equipment, records, facilities, fish and fish products and any relevant documents necessary to verify compliance with the relevant conservation and management measures.

3. The flag State shall ensure that vessel masters:

(a) accept and facilitate prompt and safe boarding by the inspectors;

(b) cooperate with and assist in the inspection of the vessel conducted pursuant to these procedures;

(c) do not obstruct, intimidate or interfere with the inspectors in the performance of their duties;

(d) allow the inspectors to communicate with the authorities of the flag State and the inspecting State during the boarding and inspection;

(e) provide reasonable facilities, including, where appropriate, food and accommodation, to the inspectors; and

(f) facilitate safe disembarkation by the inspectors.

4. In the event that the master of a vessel refuses to accept boarding and inspection in accordance with this article and article 21, the flag State shall, except in circumstances where, in accordance with generally accepted international regulations, procedures and practices relating to safety at sea, it is necessary to delay the boarding and inspection, direct the master of the vessel to submit immediately to boarding and inspection and, if the master does not comply with such direction, shall suspend the vessel's authorization to fish and order the vessel to return immediately to port. The flag State shall advise the inspecting State of the action it has taken when the circumstances referred to in this paragraph arise.

Article 23
Measures taken by a port State

1. A port State has the right and the duty to take measures, in accordance with international law, to promote the effectiveness of subregional, regional and global conservation and management measures. When taking such measures a port State shall not discriminate in form or in fact against the vessels of any State.
2. A port State may, inter alia, inspect documents, fishing gear and catch on board fishing vessels, when such vessels are voluntarily in its ports or at its offshore terminals.
3. States may adopt regulations empowering the relevant national authorities to prohibit landings and transshipments where it has been established that the catch has been taken in a manner which undermines the effectiveness of subregional, regional or global conservation and management measures on the high seas.
4. Nothing in this article affects the exercise by States of their sovereignty over ports in their territory in accordance with international law.

Part VII
Requirements of Developing States

Article 24
Recognition of the special requirements of developing States

1. States shall give full recognition to the special requirements of developing States in relation to conservation and management of straddling fish stocks and highly migratory fish stocks and development of fisheries for such stocks. To this end, States shall, either directly or through the United Nations Development Programme, the Food and Agriculture Organization of the United Nations and other specialized agencies, the Global Environment Facility, the Commission on Sustainable Development and other appropriate international and regional organizations and bodies, provide assistance to developing States.
2. In giving effect to the duty to cooperate in the establishment of conservation and management measures for straddling fish stocks and highly

migratory fish stocks, States shall take into account the special requirements of developing States, in particular:

(a) the vulnerability of developing States which are dependent on the
exploitation of living marine resources, including for meeting the
nutritional requirements of their populations or parts thereof;

(b) the need to avoid adverse impacts on, and ensure access to fisheries
by, subsistence, small-scale and artisanal fishers and women fish-
workers, as well as indigenous people in developing States, particularly small island developing States; and

(c) the need to ensure that such measures do not result in transferring,
directly or indirectly, a disproportionate burden of conservation action onto developing States.

Article 25
Forms of cooperation with developing States

1. States shall cooperate, either directly or through subregional, regional or
global organizations:

(a) to enhance the ability of developing States, in particular the least-
developed among them and small island developing States, to conserve and manage straddling fish stocks and highly migratory fish
stocks and to develop their own fisheries for such stocks;

(b) to assist developing States, in particular the least-developed among
them and small island developing States, to enable them to participate in high seas fisheries for such stocks, including facilitating access to such fisheries subject to articles 5 and 11; and

(c) to facilitate the participation of developing States in subregional and
regional fisheries management organizations and arrangements.

2. Cooperation with developing States for the purposes set out in this article shall include the provision of financial assistance, assistance relating
to human resources development, technical assistance, transfer of technology, including through joint venture arrangements, and advisory and
consultative services.

3. Such assistance shall, inter alia, be directed specifically towards:

(a) improved conservation and management of straddling fish stocks and
highly migratory fish stocks through collection, reporting, verification, exchange and analysis of fisheries data and related information;

(b) stock assessment and scientific research; and

(c) monitoring, control, surveillance, compliance and enforcement, including training and capacity-building at the local level, development and funding of national and regional observer programmes and access to technology and equipment.

Article 26
Special assistance in the implementation of this Agreement

1. States shall cooperate to establish special funds to assist developing States in the implementation of this Agreement, including assisting developing States to meet the costs involved in any proceedings for the settlement of disputes to which they may be parties.

2. States and international organizations should assist developing States in establishing new subregional or regional fisheries management organizations or arrangements, or in strengthening existing organizations or arrangements, for the conservation and management of straddling fish stocks and highly migratory fish stocks.

Part VIII
Peaceful Settlement of Disputes

Article 27
Obligation to settle disputes by peaceful means

States have the obligation to settle their disputes by negotiation, inquiry, mediation, conciliation, arbitration, judicial settlement, resort to regional agencies or arrangements, or other peaceful means of their own choice.

Article 28
Prevention of disputes

States shall cooperate in order to prevent disputes. To this end, States shall agree on efficient and expeditious decision-making procedures within subregional and regional fisheries management organizations and arrangements and shall strengthen existing decision-making procedures as necessary.

Article 29
Disputes of a technical nature

Where a dispute concerns a matter of a technical nature, the States concerned may refer the dispute to an ad hoc expert panel established by them. The panel shall confer with the States concerned and shall endeavour to resolve the dispute expeditiously without recourse to binding procedures for the settlement of disputes.

Article 30
Procedures for the settlement of disputes

1. The provisions relating to the settlement of disputes set out in Part XV of the Convention apply mutatis mutandis to any dispute between States Parties to this Agreement concerning the interpretation or application of this Agreement, whether or not they are also Parties to the Convention.

2. The provisions relating to the settlement of disputes set out in Part XV of the Convention apply mutatis mutandis to any dispute between States Parties to this Agreement concerning the interpretation or application of a subregional, regional or global fisheries agreement relating to straddling fish stocks or highly migratory fish stocks to which they are parties, including any dispute concerning the conservation and management of such stocks, whether or not they are also Parties to the Convention.

3. Any procedure accepted by a State Party to this Agreement and the Convention pursuant to article 287 of the Convention shall apply to the settlement of disputes under this Part, unless that State Party, when signing, ratifying or acceding to this Agreement, or at any time thereafter, has accepted another procedure pursuant to article 287 for the settlement of disputes under this Part.

4. A State Party to this Agreement which is not a Party to the Convention, when signing, ratifying or acceding to this Agreement, or at any time thereafter, shall be free to choose, by means of a written declaration, one or more of the means set out in article 287, paragraph 1, of the Convention for the settlement of disputes under this Part. Article 287 shall apply to such a declaration, as well as to any dispute to which such State is a party which is not covered by a declaration in force. For the purposes of conciliation and arbitration in accordance with Annexes V, VII and VIII to the Convention, such State shall be entitled to nominate conciliators, arbitrators and experts to be included in the lists referred to in Annex V, article 2, Annex VII, article 2, and Annex VIII, article 2, for the settlement of disputes under this Part.

5. Any court or tribunal to which a dispute has been submitted under this Part shall apply the relevant provisions of the Convention, of this Agreement and of any relevant subregional, regional or global fisheries agreement, as well as generally accepted standards for the conservation and management of living marine resources and other rules of international law not incompatible with the Convention, with a view to ensuring the conservation of the straddling fish stocks and highly migratory fish stocks concerned.

Article 31
Provisional measures

1. Pending the settlement of a dispute in accordance with this Part, the parties to the dispute shall make every effort to enter into provisional arrangements of a practical nature.
2. Without prejudice to article 290 of the Convention, the court or tribunal to which the dispute has been submitted under this Part may prescribe any provisional measures which it considers appropriate under the circumstances to preserve the respective rights of the parties to the dispute or to prevent damage to the stocks in question, as well as in the circumstances referred to in article 7, paragraph 5, and article 16, paragraph 2.
3. A State Party to this Agreement which is not a Party to the Convention may declare that, notwithstanding article 290, paragraph 5, of the Convention, the International Tribunal for the Law of the Sea shall not be entitled to prescribe, modify or revoke provisional measures without the agreement of such State.

Article 32
Limitations on applicability of procedures for the settlement of disputes
Article 297, paragraph 3, of the Convention applies also to this Agreement.

Part IX
Non-Parties to This Agreement

Article 33
Non-parties to this Agreement

1. States Parties shall encourage non-parties to this Agreement to become parties thereto and to adopt laws and regulations consistent with its provisions.

2. States Parties shall take measures consistent with this Agreement and international law to deter the activities of vessels flying the flag of non-parties which undermine the effective implementation of this Agreement.

Part X
Good Faith and Abuse of Rights

Article 34
Good faith and abuse of rights

States Parties shall fulfil in good faith the obligations assumed under this Agreement and shall exercise the rights recognized in this Agreement in a manner which would not constitute an abuse of right.

PART XI
Responsibility and Liability

Article 35
Responsibility and liability

States Parties are liable in accordance with international law for damage or loss attributable to them in regard to this Agreement.

Part XII
Review Conference

Article 36
Review conference

1. Four years after the date of entry into force of this Agreement, the Secretary-General of the United Nations shall convene a conference with a view to assessing the effectiveness of this Agreement in securing the conservation and management of straddling fish stocks and highly migratory fish stocks. The Secretary-General shall invite to the conference all States Parties and those States and entities which are entitled to become parties to this Agreement as well as those intergovernmental and non-governmental organizations entitled to participate as observers.
2. The conference shall review and assess the adequacy of the provisions of

this Agreement and, if necessary, propose means of strengthening the substance and methods of implementation of those provisions in order better to address any continuing problems in the conservation and management of straddling fish stocks and highly migratory fish stocks.

Part XIII
Final Provisions

Article 37
Signature

This Agreement shall be open for signature by all States and the other entities referred to in article 1, paragraph 2(b), and shall remain open for signature at United Nations Headquarters for twelve months from the fourth of December 1995.

Article 38
Ratification

This Agreement is subject to ratification by States and the other entities referred to in article 1, paragraph 2(b). The instruments of ratification shall be deposited with the Secretary-General of the United Nations.

Article 39
Accession

This Agreement shall remain open for accession by States and the other entities referred to in article 1, paragraph 2(b). The instruments of accession shall be deposited with the Secretary-General of the United Nations.

Article 40
Entry into force

1. This Agreement shall enter into force 30 days after the date of deposit of the thirtieth instrument of ratification or accession.
2. For each State or entity which ratifies the Agreement or accedes thereto after the deposit of the thirtieth instrument of ratification or accession, this Agreement shall enter into force on the thirtieth day following the deposit of its instrument of ratification or accession.

Article 41

Provisional application

1. This Agreement shall be applied provisionally by a State or entity which consents to its provisional application by so notifying the depositary in writing. Such provisional application shall become effective from the date of receipt of the notification.

2. Provisional application by a State or entity shall terminate upon the entry into force of this Agreement for that State or entity or upon notification by that State or entity to the depositary in writing of its intention to terminate provisional application.

Article 42

Reservations and exceptions

No reservations or exceptions may be made to this Agreement.

Article 43

Declarations and statements

Article 42 does not preclude a State or entity, when signing, ratifying or acceding to this Agreement, from making declarations or statements, however phrased or named, with a view, inter alia, to the harmonization of its laws and regulations with the provisions of this Agreement, provided that such declarations or statements do not purport to exclude or to modify the legal effect of the provisions of this Agreement in their application to that State or entity.

Article 44

Relation to other agreements

1. This Agreement shall not alter the rights and obligations of States Parties which arise from other agreements compatible with this Agreement and which do not affect the enjoyment by other States Parties of their rights or the performance of their obligations under this Agreement.

2. Two or more States Parties may conclude agreements modifying or suspending the operation of provisions of this Agreement, applicable solely to the relations between them, provided that such agreements do not relate to a provision derogation from which is incompatible with the effective execution of the object and purpose of this Agreement, and provid-

ed further that such agreements shall not affect the application of the basic principles embodied herein, and that the provisions of such agreements do not affect the enjoyment by other States Parties of their rights or the performance of their obligations under this Agreement.

3. States Parties intending to conclude an agreement referred to in paragraph 2 shall notify the other States Parties through the depositary of this Agreement of their intention to conclude the agreement and of the modification or suspension for which it provides.

Article 45
Amendment

1. A State Party may, by written communication addressed to the Secretary-General of the United Nations, propose amendments to this Agreement and request the convening of a conference to consider such proposed amendments. The Secretary-General shall circulate such communication to all States Parties. If, within six months from the date of the circulation of the communication, not less than one half of the States Parties reply favourably to the request, the Secretary-General shall convene the conference.

2. The decision-making procedure applicable at the amendment conference convened pursuant to paragraph 1 shall be the same as that applicable at the United Nations Conference on Straddling Fish Stocks and Highly Migratory Fish Stocks, unless otherwise decided by the conference. The conference should make every effort to reach agreement on any amendments by way of consensus and there should be no voting on them until all efforts at consensus have been exhausted.

3. Once adopted, amendments to this Agreement shall be open for signature at United Nations Headquarters by States Parties for twelve months from the date of adoption, unless otherwise provided in the amendment itself.

4. Articles 38, 39, 47 and 50 apply to all amendments to this Agreement.

5. Amendments to this Agreement shall enter into force for the States Parties ratifying or acceding to them on the thirtieth day following the deposit of instruments of ratification or accession by two thirds of the States Parties. Thereafter, for each State Party ratifying or acceding to an amendment after the deposit of the required number of such instruments, the

amendment shall enter into force on the thirtieth day following the deposit of its instrument of ratification or accession.

6   An amendment may provide that a smaller or a larger number of ratifications or accessions shall be required for its entry into force than are required by this article.

7.   A State which becomes a Party to this Agreement after the entry into force of amendments in accordance with paragraph 5 shall, failing an expression of a different intention by that State:

(a)   be considered as a Party to this Agreement as so amended; and

(b)   be considered as a Party to the unamended Agreement in relation to any State Party not bound by the amendment.

Article 46

Denunciation

1.   A State Party may, by written notification addressed to the Secretary-General of the United Nations, denounce this Agreement and may indicate its reasons. Failure to indicate reasons shall not affect the validity of the denunciation. The denunciation shall take effect one year after the date of receipt of the notification, unless the notification specifies a later date.

2.   The denunciation shall not in any way affect the duty of any State Party to fulfil any obligation embodied in this Agreement to which it would be subject under international law independently of this Agreement.

Article 47

Participation by international organizations

1.   In cases where an international organization referred to in Annex IX, article 1, of the Convention does not have competence over all the matters governed by this Agreement, Annex IX to the Convention shall apply mutatis mutandis to participation by such international organization in this Agreement, except that the following provisions of that Annex shall not apply:

(a)   article 2, first sentence; and

(b)   article 3, paragraph 1.

2.   In cases where an international organization referred to in Annex IX, article 1, of the Convention has competence over all the matters governed by this Agreement, the following provisions shall apply to participation by such international organization in this Agreement:

(a) at the time of signature or accession, such international organization shall make a declaration stating:

    (i) that it has competence over all the matters governed by this Agreement;

    (ii) that, for this reason, its member States shall not become States Parties, except in respect of their territories for which the international organization has no responsibility; and

    (iii) that it accepts the rights and obligations of States under this Agreement;

(b) participation of such an international organization shall in no case confer any rights under this Agreement on member States of the international organization;

(c) in the event of a conflict between the obligations of an international organization under this Agreement and its obligations under the agreement establishing the international organization or any acts relating to it, the obligations under this Agreement shall prevail.

Article 48
Annexes

1. The Annexes form an integral part of this Agreement and, unless expressly provided otherwise, a reference to this Agreement or to one of its Parts includes a reference to the Annexes relating thereto.

2. The Annexes may be revised from time to time by States Parties. Such revisions shall be based on scientific and technical considerations. Notwithstanding the provisions of article 45, if a revision to an Annex is adopted by consensus at a meeting of States Parties, it shall be incorporated in this Agreement and shall take effect from the date of its adoption or from such other date as may be specified in the revision. If a revision to an Annex is not adopted by consensus at such a meeting, the amendment procedures set out in article 45 shall apply.

Article 49
Depositary

The Secretary-General of the United Nations shall be the depositary of this Agreement and any amendments or revisions thereto.

Article 50
Authentic texts

The Arabic, Chinese, English, French, Russian and Spanish texts of this Agreement are equally authentic.

IN WITNESS WHEREOF, the undersigned Plenipotentiaries, being duly authorized thereto, have signed this Agreement.

OPENED FOR SIGNATURE at New York, this fourth day of December, one thousand nine hundred and ninety-five, in a single original, in the Arabic, Chinese, English, French, Russian and Spanish languages.

Annex I
Standard Requirements for the Collection and Sharing of Data

Article 1
General principles

1. The timely collection, compilation and analysis of data are fundamental to the effective conservation and management of straddling fish stocks and highly migratory fish stocks. To this end, data from fisheries for these stocks on the high seas and those in areas under national jurisdiction are required and should be collected and compiled in such a way as to enable statistically meaningful analysis for the purposes of fishery resource conservation and management. These data include catch and fishing effort statistics and other fishery-related information, such as vessel-related and other data for standardizing fishing effort. Data collected should also include information on non-target and associated or dependent species. All data should be verified to ensure accuracy. Confidentiality of non-aggregated data shall be maintained. The dissemination of such data shall be subject to the terms on which they have been provided.

2. Assistance, including training as well as financial and technical assistance, shall be provided to developing States in order to build capacity in the field of conservation and management of living marine resources. Assistance should focus on enhancing capacity to implement data collection and verification, observer programmes, data analysis and research

projects supporting stock assessments. The fullest possible involvement of developing State scientists and managers in conservation and management of straddling fish stocks and highly migratory fish stocks should be promoted.

Article 2
Principles of data collection, compilation and exchange
The following general principles should be considered in defining the parameters for collection, compilation and exchange of data from fishing operations for straddling fish stocks and highly migratory fish stocks:

(a) States should ensure that data are collected from vessels flying their flag on fishing activities according to the operational characteristics of each fishing method (e.g., each individual tow for trawl, each set for long-line and purse-seine, each school fished for pole-and-line and each day fished for troll) and in sufficient detail to facilitate effective stock assessment;

(b) States should ensure that fishery data are verified through an appropriate system;

(c) States should compile fishery-related and other supporting scientific data and provide them in an agreed format and in a timely manner to the relevant subregional or regional fisheries management organization or arrangement where one exists. Otherwise, States should cooperate to exchange data either directly or through such other cooperative mechanisms as may be agreed among them;

(d) States should agree, within the framework of subregional or regional fisheries management organizations or arrangements, or otherwise, on the specification of data and the format in which they are to be provided, in accordance with this Annex and taking into account the nature of the stocks and the fisheries for those stocks in the region. Such organizations or arrangements should request non-members or non-participants to provide data concerning relevant fishing activities by vessels flying their flag;

(e) such organizations or arrangements shall compile data and make them available in a timely manner and in an agreed format to all interested States under the terms and conditions established by the organization or arrangement; and

(f)   scientists of the flag State and from the relevant subregional or regional fisheries management organization or arrangement should analyse the data separately or jointly, as appropriate.

Article 3
Basic fishery data

1. States shall collect and make available to the relevant subregional or regional fisheries management organization or arrangement the following types of data in sufficient detail to facilitate effective stock assessment in accordance with agreed procedures:

    (a)   time series of catch and effort statistics by fishery and fleet;

    (b)   total catch in number, nominal weight, or both, by species (both target and non-target) as is appropriate to each fishery. [Nominal weight is defined by the Food and Agriculture Organization of the United Nations as the live-weight equivalent of the landings];

    (c)   discard statistics, including estimates where necessary, reported as number or nominal weight by species, as is appropriate to each fishery;

    (d)   effort statistics appropriate to each fishing method; and

    (e)   fishing location, date and time fished and other statistics on fishing operations as appropriate.

2.   States shall also collect where appropriate and provide to the relevant subregional or regional fisheries management organization or arrangement information to support stock assessment, including:

    (a)   composition of the catch according to length, weight and sex;

    (b)   other biological information supporting stock assessments, such as information on age, growth, recruitment, distribution and stock identity; and

    (c)   other relevant research, including surveys of abundance, biomass surveys, hydro-acoustic surveys, research on environmental factors affecting stock abundance, and oceanographic and ecological studies.

Article 4
Vessel data and information

1.   States should collect the following types of vessel-related data for standardizing fleet composition and vessel fishing power and for converting between different measures of effort in the analysis of catch and effort data:

(a) vessel identification, flag and port of registry;

(b) vessel type;

(c) vessel specifications (e.g., material of construction, date built, registered length, gross registered tonnage, power of main engines, hold capacity and catch storage methods); and

(d) fishing gear description (e.g., types, gear specifications and quantity).

2. The flag State will collect the following information:

(a) navigation and position fixing aids;

(b) communication equipment and international radio call sign; and

(c) crew size.

Article 5

Reporting

A State shall ensure that vessels flying its flag send to its national fisheries administration and, where agreed, to the relevant subregional or regional fisheries management organization or arrangement, logbook data on catch and effort, including data on fishing operations on the high seas, at sufficiently frequent intervals to meet national requirements and regional and international obligations. Such data shall be transmitted, where necessary, by radio, telex, facsimile or satellite transmission or by other means.

Article 6

Data verification

States or, as appropriate, subregional or regional fisheries management organizations or arrangements should establish mechanisms for verifying fishery data, such as:

(a) position verification through vessel monitoring systems;

(b) scientific observer programmes to monitor catch, effort, catch composition (target and non-target) and other details of fishing operations;

(c) vessel trip, landing and transshipment reports; and

(d) port sampling.

Article 7

Data exchange

1. Data collected by flag States must be shared with other flag States and relevant coastal States through appropriate subregional or regional fisheries

management organizations or arrangements. Such organizations or arrangements shall compile data and make them available in a timely manner and in an agreed format to all interested States under the terms and conditions established by the organization or arrangement, while maintaining confidentiality of non-aggregated data, and should, to the extent feasible, develop database systems which provide efficient access to data.

2. At the global level, collection and dissemination of data should be effected through the Food and Agriculture Organization of the United Nations. Where a subregional or regional fisheries management organization or arrangement does not exist, that organization may also do the same at the subregional or regional level by arrangement with the States concerned.

Annex II

Guidelines for the Application of Precautionary Reference Points in Conservation and Management of Straddling Fish Stocks and Highly Migratory Fish Stocks

1. A precautionary reference point is an estimated value derived through an agreed scientific procedure, which corresponds to the state of the resource and of the fishery, and which can be used as a guide for fisheries management.

2. Two types of precautionary reference points should be used: conservation, or limit, reference points and management, or target, reference points. Limit reference points set boundaries which are intended to constrain harvesting within safe biological limits within which the stocks can produce maximum sustainable yield. Target reference points are intended to meet management objectives.

3. Precautionary reference points should be stock-specific to account, inter alia, for the reproductive capacity, the resilience of each stock and the characteristics of fisheries exploiting the stock, as well as other sources of mortality and major sources of uncertainty.

4. Management strategies shall seek to maintain or restore populations of harvested stocks, and where necessary associated or dependent species, at levels consistent with previously agreed precautionary reference points. Such reference points shall be used to trigger pre-agreed conser-

vation and management action. Management strategies shall include measures which can be implemented when precautionary reference points are approached.

5. Fishery management strategies shall ensure that the risk of exceeding limit reference points is very low. If a stock falls below a limit reference point or is at risk of falling below such a reference point, conservation and management action should be initiated to facilitate stock recovery. Fishery management strategies shall ensure that target reference points are not exceeded on average.

6. When information for determining reference points for a fishery is poor or absent, provisional reference points shall be set. Provisional reference points may be established by analogy to similar and better-known stocks. In such situations, the fishery shall be subject to enhanced monitoring so as to enable revision of provisional reference points as improved information becomes available.

7. The fishing mortality rate which generates maximum sustainable yield should be regarded as a minimum standard for limit reference points. For stocks which are not overfished, fishery management strategies shall ensure that fishing mortality does not exceed that which corresponds to maximum sustainable yield, and that the biomass does not fall below a predefined threshold. For overfished stocks, the biomass which would produce maximum sustainable yield can serve as a rebuilding target.

APPENDIX III

The FAO Standard Specifications for the Marking and Identification of Fishing Vessels

CONTENTS

FOREWORD

The need for an international standard system for the marking and identification of fishing vessels was included in the Strategy for Fisheries Management and Development approved by the 1984 FAO World Fisheries Conference. An Expert Consultation on the Marking of Fishing Vessels convened by the Government of Canada, in collaboration with FAO, in Halifax, Nova Scotia, Canada, March 1985, elaborated the basis for a standard system.

A review of the report of this Expert Consultation by the Sixteenth Session of the FAO Committee on Fisheries resulted in a further Expert Consultation on the Technical Specifications for the Marking of Fishing Vessels convened in Rome, June 1986.

The Specifications contained herein were endorsed by the Eighteenth Session of the FAO Committee on Fisheries, Rome, April 1989, for adoption by States on a voluntary basis as a standard system to identify fishing vessels operating, or likely to operate, in waters of States other than those of the flag State. The Director General of FAO has informed the Secretary Generals of the International Maritime Organization (IMO) and the International Telecommunication Union (ITU) of the adoption of these Standard Specifications as an aid to fisheries management and safety at sea.

1. GENERAL PROVISIONS
1.1 Purpose and scope

    1.1.1 As an aid to fisheries management and safety at sea, fishing vessels should be appropriately marked for their identification on the basis of the International Telecommunication Union Radio Call Signs (IRCS) system.

    1.1.2 For the purpose of these Standard Specifications, the use of the word "vessel" refers to any vessel intending to fish or engaged in fishing or ancillary activities, operating, or likely to operate, in waters of States other than those of the flag State.

1.2 Definitions

For the purpose of these Specifications:

    a)   the word "vessel" also includes a boat, skiff or craft (excluding aircraft) carried on board another vessel and required for fishing operations;

    b)   a deck is any surface lying in the horizontal plane, including the top of the wheelhouse;

c)   a radio station is one that is assigned an International Tele-communication Union Radio Call Sign.

1.3 Basis for the Standard Specifications

The basis for the Standard Specifications, the IRCS system, meets the following requirements:

a)   the use of an established international system from which the identity and nationality of vessels can be readily determined, irrespective of size and tonnage, and for which a register is maintained;

b)   it is without prejudice to international conventions, national or bilateral practices;

c)   implementation and maintenance will be at minimum cost to governments and vessel owners; and,

d)   it facilitates search and rescue operations.

2.   BASIC SYSTEM AND APPLICATION

2.1 Basic system

2.1.1 The Standard Specifications are based on:

a)   the International Telecommunication Union's system for the allocation of signs to countries for ship stations; and,

b)   generally accepted design standards for lettering and numbering.

2.1.2 Vessels shall be marked with their International Telecommunication Union Radio Call Signs (IRCS).

2.1.3 Except as provided for in paragraph 2.2.6 below, vessels to which an IRCS has not been assigned shall be marked with the characters allocated by the, International Telecommunication Union (ITU) to the flag State and followed by, as appropriate, the licence or registration number assigned by the flag State. In such cases, a hyphen shall be placed between the nationality identification characters and the licence or registration number identifying the vessel.

2.1.4 In order to avoid confusion with the letters I and 0 it is recommended that numbers 1 and 0, which are specifically excluded from the ITU call signs, be avoided by national authorities when allocating licence or registration numbers.

2.1.5 Apart from the vessels name or identification mark and the port of registry required by international practice or national legislation, the marking system as specified shall, in order to avoid confusion, be the only other vessel identification mark consisting of letters and numbers to be painted on the hull or superstructure.

2.2 Application

2.2.1 The markings shall be prominently displayed at all times:

    a)   on the vessel's side or superstructure, port and starboard; fixtures inclined at an angle to the vessel's side or superstructure would be considered as suitable provided that the angle of inclination would not prevent sighting of the sign from another vessel or from the air;

    b)   on a deck, except as provided for in paragraph 2.2.4 below. Should an awning or other temporary cover be placed so as to obscure the mark on a deck, the awning or cover shall also be marked. These marks should be placed athwartships with the top of the numbers or letters towards the bow.

2.2.2 Marks should be placed as high as possible above the waterline on both sides. Such parts of the hull as the flare of the bow and the stern shall be avoided.

2.2.3 The marks shall:

    a)   be so placed that they are not obscured by the fishing gear whether it is stowed or in use;

    b)   be clear of flow from scuppers or overboard discharges including areas which might be prone to damage or discolouration from the catch of certain types of species; and,

    c)   not extend below the waterline.

2.2.4 Undecked vessels shall not be required to display the markings on a horizontal surface. However, owners should be encouraged, where practical, to fit a board on which the markings may be clearly seen from the air.

2.2.5 Vessels fitted with sails may display the markings on the sail in addition to the hull.

2.2.6 Boats, skiffs and craft carried by the vessel for fishing operations shall bear the same mark as the vessel concerned.

2.2.7 Examples of the placement of marks are set out in pages 47 to 69 of the FAO publication "The Standard Specifications for the Marking and Identification of Fishing Vessels".

3. TECHNICAL SPECIFICATIONS

3.1 Specifications of letters and numbers

3.1.1 Block lettering and numbering shall be used throughout.

3.1.2 The width of the letters and numbers shall be in proportion to the height.

3.1.3 The height (h) of the letters and numbers shall be in proportion to the size of the vessel in accordance with the following:

a) for marks to be placed on the hull, superstructure and/or inclined surfaces:

Length of vessel overall (LOA) in meters (m)	*Height of letters and numbers in meters (m) to be less than:*
25 m and over	1.0 m
20 m but less than 25 m	0.8 m
15 m but less than 20 m	0.6 m
12 m but less than 15 m	0.4 m
5 m but less than 12 m	0.3 m
Under 5 m	0.1 m

b) for marks to be placed on deck: the height shall not be less than 0.3 m for all classes of vessels of 5 m and over.

3.1.4 The length of the hyphen shall be half the height of the letters and numbers.

3.1.5 The width of the stroke for all letters, numbers and the hyphen shall be

3.1.6 Spacing:

a) the space between letters and/or numbers shall not exceed- nor be less than $h/6$

b) the space between adjacent letters having sloping sides shall not exceed $h/8$

nor be less than $h/10$

for example A V.

3.2 Painting

3.2.1 The marks shall be:

    a)   white on a black background; or,

    b)   black on a white background.

3.2.2 The background shall extend to provide a border around the mark of not less than $h/6$.

3.2.3 Good quality marine paints to be used throughout.

3.2.4 The use of retro-reflective or heat-generating substances shall be accepted, provided that the mark meets the requirements of these Standard Specifications.

3.2.5 The marks and the background shall be maintained in good condition at all times.

4. REGISTRATION OF MARKS

4.1 The International Telecommunication Union maintains and updates a worldwide register of International Radio Call Signs that contains details of the nationality of the vessel and its name.

4.2 In addition to maintaining a separate register of its vessels., which IRCS have been assigned, the flag State shall also maintain a record of vessels to which it has given a nationality identifier (allocated by the ITU), followed by the hyphen and licence/registration number; such records should include details of the vessels and owners.

5. INTERNATIONAL ALLOCATION OF CALL SIGNS

5.1 The International Telecommunication Union (ITU) Geneva allocates call signs to countries. These take the form of letters of the alphabet or number and letters, for example:

- one of the sets of call signs allocated to Italy is **LAA-IZZ** inclusive, whereas,
- one of the sets allocated to Malaysia is **9WA-9WZ.**

5.2 These signs allocated by the ITU clearly identify the flag State. The flag State adds further characters to the allocated call sign in order to identify the "radio station" (the vessel). A typical example being JNQK which is a Japanese vessel.

5.3 ITU should be contacted for an update of the List of Call Signs.

NOTES

Introduction

1. Agenda 21, paragraph 17.49(e).
2. Agenda 21, paragraph 17.52.53.
3. Edeson, William. 1996. "The Code of Conduct for Responsible Fisheries: An Introduction." *International Journal of Marine and Coastal Law* 11: 97.
4. In its first versions, the Compliance Agreement was meant to deal directly with the act of re-flagging, by providing "that parties to the agreement should refuse to register fishing vessels unless they had sufficient grounds to believe that the vessel would not be used to undermine the effectiveness of internationally agreed conservation and management measures." It soon became clear, however, that general consent would not be reached on any such agreement and for this reason, the primary focus of the draft agreement was changed from the legal act of flagging and vessel registration to the act of authorizing a vessel to fish on the high seas. Moore, Gerald. 1995. "The Food and Agriculture Organization Compliance Agreement." *International Journal of Marine and Coastal Law* 10: 412–16, at 412.
5. Article 2 of the Compliance Agreement.

Part One: Implementing the Compliance Agreement

6. The agreement was approved by the FAO conference on 24 November 1993, under Article XIV of the FAO constitution. It is open to acceptance by any member or associate member of FAO, and to any non-member state that is a member of the United Nations, or of any of the specialized agencies of the United Nations or of the International Atomic Energy Agency. It has been accepted by the following: Canada, 20 May 1994; Saint Kitts and Nevis, 24 June 1994; Georgia, 7 September 1994; Myanmar, 8 September 1994; Sweden, 25 October 1994; Madagascar, 26 October 1994; Norway, 28 December 1994; United States of America, 19 December 1995; Argentina, 24 June 1996; European Community, 6 August 1996; Namibia, 7 August 1998; Benin, 4 January 1999; Tanzania, 17 February 1999; Mexico, 11 March 1999; Uruguay, 11 November 1999; Seychelles, 7 April 2000; Japan, 20 June 2000; Cyprus, 19 July 2000; and Barbados, 26 October 2000.

7. In many common law jurisdictions the chief fisheries officer, the director of fisheries, or someone in a similar position would be appointed to carry out the administration of such responsibilities.

8. "Guidelines for the Implementation in National Legislation of the Agreement to Promote Compliance with International Conservation and Management Measures by Fishing Vessels on the High Seas" (FAO Guidelines) was published by the FAO Legal Office, 1994. See pp. 29–30.

9. The concept of the responsibility of the flag state for the activities of its fishing vessels was first put forward in the World Fisheries Strategy adopted by the FAO World Conference on Fisheries Management and Development held in Rome in 1984. Since then some aspects of flag state responsibility have been taken up in bilateral agreements, but never before in an agreement of global application. Moore (1995: 413–15). See note 4 above for full reference.

10. Article III.2 of the Compliance Agreement.

11. Section 104(c) of the U.S. High Seas Fishing Compliance Act of 1995.

12. FAO Guidelines (1994: 6 *n.* 4). See note 8 for publication information.

13. Section 104(4) of the U.S. High Seas Fishing Compliance Act.

14. Section 41(1) of the Marine Living Resources Act of the Republic of South Africa.

15. OECS 1997 Workshop Report, p. 17.

16. The responsibilities of a flag state are elaborated on in the International Plan of Action on Illegal Unreported and Unregulated Fishing," agreed upon at COFI, Rome, March 2001. See in particular paragraphs 34 to 50.

17. Article III.5 of the Compliance Agreement.

18. Article III.6 of the Compliance Agreement.

19. Article III.7 of the Compliance Agreement.

20. Article III.8 of the Compliance Agreement.

21. Section 52 of the Marine Living Resources Act of the Republic of South Africa.

22. Sections 107–110 of the U.S. High Seas Fishing Compliance Act.

23. Article IV of the Compliance Agreement.

24. The term "record" is defined in the Compliance Agreement to mean "a record of fishing vessels in which are recorded pertinent details of the fishing vessel. It may constitute a separate record for fishing vessels or form part of a general record of fishing vessels."

25. Section 12 of the Marine Living Resources Act of the Republic of South Africa.

26. Article VI.1 of the Compliance Agreement.

The information required is as follows:

a) name of fishing vessel, registration number, previous names (if known), and port of registry;

b) previous flag (if any);

c) International Radio Call Sign (if any);

d) name and address of owner or owners;

e) where and when built;

f) type of vessel; and

g) length.

27. Article VI.2 of the Compliance Agreement.

The additional information is as follows:

a) name and address of operator (manager) or operators (managers) (if any);

b) type of fishing method or methods;

c) moulded depth;

d) beam;

e) gross register tonnage; and

f) power of main engine or engines.

28. Article VI.3 of the Compliance Agreement.

29. Article VI.5 of the Compliance Agreement.

30. Article VI.10 of the Compliance Agreement.

31. Subject to any restrictions imposed by the party concerned regarding the distribution of information.

32. Article VI.4 of the Compliance Agreement.

33. Article VI.8(a) of the Compliance Agreement.

34. Article VI.8(b) of the Compliance Agreement.

35. Article VI(9) of the Compliance Agreement.

36. Article VI.4.

37. For a discussion of this, see R. Grainger, "High Seas Fishing Vessel Database." In Myron H. Nordquist and John Norton Moore (eds.), *Current Fisheries Issues and the Food and Agriculture Organization of the United Nations*, Martinus Nijhoff, The Hague, 2000.

38. OECS 1997 Workshop Report, p. 19.

39. Edeson, William. "Towards Long Term Sustainable Use: Some Recent Developments in the Legal Regime of Fisheries" in Alan Boyle and David Freestone (eds.) *International Law and Sustainable Development: Past Achievements and Future Challenges,* Oxford, 1999.

The preamble to the Compliance Agreement does, however, say:

"The Parties to the Agreement . . . *conscious* of the duties of every State to exercise effectively its jurisdiction and control over vessels flying its flag, including fishing vessels and vessels engaged in the **transshipment** of fish. . . have agreed as follows. . . ."

40. Article II.2 of the Compliance Agreement.

41. Article II.3 of the Compliance Agreement.

42. Regulation 68 of the Canadian Coastal Fisheries Protection Act.

43. Regulation 65 of the Canadian Coastal Fisheries Protection Act. Regulation 66 also prohibits a Canadian vessel in waters under the jurisdiction of the United States from having any fishing gear on board unless it is stored below deck or is otherwise removed from the place where it is normally used for fishing and is not otherwise readily available for fishing.

44. See "The Norwegian Experience in Implementing the 1993 FAO Compliance Agreement and the 1995 UN Fish Stocks Agreement," by Sigmund Engessaetter, Directorate of Fisheries, Bergen, Norway, paper presented at the FAO/OECS Regional Workshop, St Lucia, July 1997.

45. We are grateful to Mr. Terje Loebach of the Directorate of Fisheries for providing us with the information on the contents of this regulation, which is currently not available in English.

46. Regulations relating to the regulation of fisheries in waters outside the fisheries jurisdiction of any state, dated 4 March 1998.

Part Two: Implementing the Fish Stocks Agreement

47. As of 31 January 2001, the countries that have ratified or acceded to the Fish Stocks Agreement are the following: Australia on 23 December 1999; Bahamas on 16 January 1997; Barbados on 22 September 2000; Brazil on 8 March 2000; Canada on 3 August 1999; Cook Islands on 1 April 1999; Fiji on 4 December 1996; Iceland on 14 February 1999; Iran on 17 April 1998; Luxembourg on 5 October 2000 (though this was subsequently declared to be premature by Luxembourg, as it is intended that all members of the European Union would deposit their instruments simultaneously: communication to the Secretary-General on 21 December 2000); Maldives on 30 December 1998; Mauritius on 25 March 1997; Federated States of Micronesia on 23 May 1997; Monaco on 9 June 1999; Namibia on 8 April 1998; Nauru on 10 January 1997; Norway on 30 December 1996; Papua New Guinea on 4 June 1999; Russian Federation on 4 August 1997, Saint Lucia on 9 August 1996; Samoa on 25 October 1996; Senegal on 30 January 1997; Seychelles on 20 March 1998; Solomon Islands on 13 February 1997; Sri Lanka on 24 October 1996; Tonga on 31 July 1996; the United States of America on 21 August 1996; and Uruguay on 10 September 1999.

48. Article 3 of the Fish Stocks Agreement.

49. Based in part on the "Harmonised OECS High Seas Fishing Law" (third draft), drafted and presented by S. Hodgson and H. Walters at the OECS/FAO Regional Workshop on the Implementation of the 1993 FAO Compliance Agreement and the 1995 UN Fish Stocks Agreement in July 1997.

50. Article 3(2) of the Fish Stocks Agreement.

51. As the OECS Workshop Report suggests, ". . . as long as regard is had to these principles in the formulation of national policy, there is no concrete need to amend national legislation. . . ." OECS draft, p. 23.

52. In Iceland, Act No. 151/1996 on Fisheries Outside the Jurisdiction of Iceland does not mention the precautionary approach directly. It does, however, clearly empower the minister to set regulations applying the precautionary approach along with other principles of the Fish Stocks Agreement. Article 7 reads as follows: "The Minister will by regulation set rules for the types and forms of fishing equipment of Icelandic vessels fishing outside Icelandic jurisdiction. . . . The Minister may also set rules on the closing of certain fishing areas and other measures that may be necessary to ensure the conservation of small fish and responsible fisheries. The Minister shall in this regard base action on international agreements to which Iceland is party. . . ."

53. One particular amendment of the Fisheries Legislation Amendment Act (Australia) is worth drawing specific attention to:

(5C) A plan of management for a fishery affecting straddling fish stocks, highly migratory fish stocks or ecologically related fish stocks (within the meaning of the Fish Stocks Agreement) must set out stock-specific reference points (within the meaning of that Agreement) for the stocks (section 17 5C).

54. No. 18/1998 of the Marine Living Resources Act of the Republic of South Africa.

55. In the Namibian Marine Resources Bill, the solution adopted has been to state the objectives of the bill broadly in the preamble: "To provide for the conservation of the marine ecosystem and the responsible utilization, conservation, protection and promotion of marine resources on a sustainable basis; for that purpose to provide for the exercise of control over marine resources; and to provide for matters connected therewith." This needs to be seen in conjunction with section 2: "The Minister may from time to time determine the general policy with regard to the conservation and utilization of marine resources in order to realize the greatest benefit for all Namibians both present and future."

56. Article 5(j) of the Fish Stocks Agreement.

57. For a discussion of the collection of fisheries data, see W. R. Edeson, 1999, "Legal Aspects of the Collection of Fisheries Data." FAO Fisheries Circular No. 953, FAO, Rome. On this issue see further below on pp. 78–81.

58. The text uses the word "approach" instead of "principle," following the terminology of Principle 15 of the 1992 UNCED Declaration. See further Ellen Hey, 1992, "The Precautionary Principle in Environmental Law and Policy: Institutionalising Caution." *Georgetown International Environmental Law Review* 4: 303–18. See also David Freestone, 1994, "The Road from Rio: International Environmental Law after the Earth Summit." *Journal of Environmental Law* 6: 193–218.

59. The concept has already been accepted in a wide range of marine environmental treaties, has been accepted in practice in agreements such as the 1994 Bering Sea Agreement and in principle in the implementation of agreements such as the Convention on the Conservation of Antarctic Marine Living Resources (CCAMLR) and the International Whaling Commission. See further David Freestone and Ellen Hey, 1996, "Implementing the Precautionary Principle: Challenges and Opportunities," in David Freestone and Ellen Hey, *The Precautionary Principle and International Law: The Challenge of Implementation,* Kluwer Law International, The Hague, 1996. *See also* Grant Hewison, 1996,"A Precautionary Approach to Fisheries Management: An Environmental Perspective." *International Journal of Marine and Coastal Law* 11: 301–30; and David Freestone, 1999, "International Fisheries Law since Rio: the Continued Rise of the Precautionary Principle," in Alan Boyle and David Freestone (eds.). *International Law and Sustainable Development: Past Achievements and Future Challenges.* Oxford, 1999.

60. The FAO Code of Conduct for Responsible Fisheries also embraces the precautionary approach as one of its general principles. Principle 6.5 of the FAO Code of Conduct reads as follows:

States and sub-regional and regional fisheries management organizations should apply a precautionary approach widely to conservation, management and exploitation of living aquatic resources in order to protect them and preserve the aquatic environment, taking account of the best scientific evidence available. The absence of adequate scientific information should not be used as a reason for postponing or failing to take measures to conserve target species, associated or dependent species and non-target species and their environment.

61. Article 6(2) of the Fish Stocks Agreement.

62. Freestone and Hey (1996), see above note 59.

63. Article 6(3)(c) of the Fish Stocks Agreement.

64. See, for example, Garcia, Serge. "The Precautionary Principle; Its Implications in Capture Fisheries Management." *Ocean and Coastal Management* 22 68 (1994), and Hewison (1996), see above note 59.

65. Davies, Peter and Catherine Redgwell. 1996. "To Conserve or to Exploit: The International Regulation of Straddling Fish Stocks." *British Yearbook of International Law*, LXVII: 199–275. The authors have vividly portrayed the methodology, using traffic light terms, as providing green and amber lights but not red. In other words, the system indicates when all is well or when dangers are threatened but does not automatically prevent fishing once the reference points are reached. The interruption or suspension of fishery operations—the "red stop light" action—still has to be determined on an ad hoc basis by the appropriate regional fisheries regulatory body.

66. See, for example, S. Garcia, above note 64; and J. Cooke and M. Earle, 1993, *Towards a Precautionary Approach to Fisheries Management*, RECIEL 2: 252.

67. See preceding discussion and also Article 6(2) of the Fish Stocks Agreement, which states the following: "The absence of adequate scientific information shall not be used as a reason for postponing or failing to take conservation and management measures." See also Article 6(3)(d) on the development of data collection and research programs, and note Article 6(6): "For new or exploratory fisheries, states shall adopt as soon as possible cautious conservation and management measures . . . [which] shall remain in force until there are sufficient data to allow assessment of the impact of the fisheries on the long-term sustainability of the stocks. . . ."

68. See Hewison (1996: 323–25), cited above in note 59. Article 6(3) seeks to require use of the best scientific information. See also discussion above. See also Article 14, and the FAO Guidelines.

69. There is some discrepancy between those who argue for a harvesting within the "natural variation" of abundance, and the traditional maximum sustainable yield approach, which is that endorsed by paragraph 7 of Annex II, but other dependent species and ecosystem factors are of course also part of the equation (see Article 6(3)(c)).

70. See Articles 6(1) and 6(5), as well as impacts of "a natural phenomenon" (Article 6(7)).

71. Here the Fish Stocks Agreement does break new ground: see Article 12 on "Transparency in activities of sub-regional and regional fisheries management organisations and arrangements."

72. FAO Fisheries Technical Paper 350/1, 1995.

73. This indeed can also happen at the international level; see further Freestone, David. 2001. "Caution or Precaution: A Rose by Any Other Name. . . ?" *Yearbook of International Environmental Law* 10: 25–32.

74. Balton, David A. 1996. "Strengthening the Law of the Sea: The New Agreement on Straddling Fish Stocks and Highly Migratory Fish Stocks." *Ocean Development & International Law* 27: 125–52, at 136. See also Balton, David. 1999, "The Compliance Agreement," in E. Hey, ed., *Developments in International Fisheries Law*, Kluwer Law International.

75. Freestone, David, and Zen Makuch. 1998. "The New International Environmental Law of Fisheries: The 1995 United Nations Straddling Stocks Agreement." *Yearbook of International Environmental Law* 7: 3–51, at 28.

76. Article 7(1)(a) of the Fish Stocks Agreement calls on relevant coastal states and states whose nationals fish for such stocks in the adjacent high seas, to "seek, either directly or through the appropriate mechanisms for cooperation . . . to agree upon the measures necessary for the conservation of [straddling fish] stocks in the adjacent high seas area."

Article 7(1)(b) targets highly migratory fish stocks and calls on relevant coastal states and other states whose nationals fish for those stocks in the region to cooperate "either directly or through the appropriate mechanisms for cooperation. . . with a view to ensuring conservation and promoting the objective of optimum utilization of such stocks throughout the region, both within and beyond the areas under national jurisdiction."

77. For general discussion, see Alex G. Oude Elferink, "The Impact of Article 7(2) of the Fish Stocks Agreement on the Formulation of Conservation and Management Measures for Straddling and Highly Migratory Fish Stocks." *FAO Papers Online* at <http://www.fao.org/legal>.

78. Article 7(2)(f) of the Fish Stocks Agreement.

79. For a discussion of the activities of these bodies, see Gail Lugten, (1999), "A Review of Measures taken by Marine Fisheries Bodies to Address Contemporary Fisheries Issues," FAO Fisheries Circular no. 940; and Judith Swan, "The Role of National Fisheries Administrations and Regional Fisheries Bodies (RFB's) in Adopting and Implementing Measures to Combat IUU Fishing," AUS:IUU/2000/4. <http://www.affa.gov.au/ecoinf/papers.html>.

80. Freestone and Makuch, above note, 75.

81. Collett, Max. 1995. "Achieving Effective International Fishery Management: A Critical Analysis of the UN Conference on Straddling Fish Stocks." *Dalhousie Journal of Legal Studies* 4: 1–33, 23–24.

82. A more detailed discussion follows.

83. As amended with section 3 of bill C-27, an "Act to amend the Coastal Fisheries Protection Act and the Canada Shipping Act to enable Canada to implement the Fish Stocks Agreement."

84. It should be pointed out, however, that this interpretation is not accepted by all parties to the negotiations. It may also be argued that, as the "Objective of the Agreement" is stated in Article 2 to be to "ensure the long-term conservation and sustainable use of straddling fish stocks and highly migratory fish stocks through effective implementation of the relevant provisions of the Convention," then, following the provisions of the Vienna Convention on the Law of Treaties, 1969, Article 31, the "objective" revealed here would possibly justify the interpretation of the agreement as being nonetheless limited to vessels engaged in fishing for the stocks to which the agreement applies.

85. Note also the definition provided in the New Zealand legislation (later in this chapter) under the heading "Jurisdiction over Nationals."

86. Article 18(3)(a) of the Fish Stocks Agreement.

87. Article 18(3)(b). An example of how this has been implemented in a different way can be found in sections 40–41 of the Marine Living Resources Act of the Republic of South Africa.

Section 40, entitled "High seas licenses," states the following:

No person shall undertake fishing or related activities on the high seas by means of a fishing vessel registered in the Republic unless a high seas fishing vessel license has been issued in respect of such a fishing vessel.

Section 41 goes on to give the minister the general power to "issue a high seas fishing license in respect of a local fishing vessel, subject to the conditions that he or she considers appropriate."

88. The member states of the Organization of Eastern Caribbean States are the following: Antigua and Barbuda, Dominica, Grenada, Montserrat, St. Lucia, St. Kitts and Nevis, and St. Vincent and the Grenadines. Associate members are the British Virgin Islands and Anguilla.

89. OECS draft, p. 26.

90. Fisheries Act of 1996, Amendment Act (No.2) of 1999, (No. 103).

91. Section 113D(2) of the Amendment Act.

92. New Zealand appears to have implemented the major provisions of the Compliance Agreement, including referring to it specifically in the legislation itself, even though at the time it had not accepted it at the international level. See sections 113E, 113F, and 113H.

93. Article 20(6) of the Fish Stocks Agreement—note, however, that this obligation requires cooperation with the coastal state, including agreement to allow the coastal state to board and inspect a vessel, even on the high seas.

94. Article 21(1) of the Fish Stocks Agreement.

95. Article 21(2) of the Fish Stocks Agreement.

96. Article 21(5) of the Fish Stocks Agreement.

97. Article 21(4) of the Fish Stocks Agreement.

98. Article 21(6)–(7). The flag state always retains the so-called right of preemption—to take over an investigation itself (Article 20(12)).

99. The Fish Stocks Agreement defines "serious violation" for these purposes and also lays down certain safeguards for the vessel being inspected. Article 21(11, 16).

100. Article 20 (6): "Where there are reasonable grounds for believing that a vessel on the high seas has been engaged in unauthorized fishing within an area under the jurisdiction of a coastal State, the flag State of that vessel, at the request of the coastal State concerned, shall immediately and fully investigate the matter. The flag State shall cooperate with the coastal State in taking appropriate enforcement action in such cases and may authorize the relevant authorities of the coastal State to board and inspect the vessel on the high seas. This paragraph is without prejudice to Article 111 of the Convention."

101. AFZ is the Australian Fishing Zone.

102. Explanatory Memorandum, Fisheries Legislation Amendment Bill (No. 1), 1999, (ISBN 0642 40845 9).

103. Article 21.14 of the Fish Stocks Agreement states the following:

This article applies mutatis mutandis to boarding and inspection by a State Party which is a member of a subregional or regional fisheries management organization or a participant in a subregional or regional fisheries management arrangement and which has clear grounds for believing that a fishing vessel flying the flag of another State Party has engaged in any activity contrary to relevant conservation and management measures referred to in paragraph 1 in the high seas area covered by such organization or arrangement, and such vessel has subsequently, during the same fishing trip, entered into an area under the national jurisdiction of the inspecting State.

104. It is important also to note amendments made to other parts of the act and to note the amendment introduced in section 105E, which provides the following:

(1) A person is guilty of an offence if:
  (a) the person intentionally uses an FSA boat; and
  (b) the person intentionally contravenes an Australian regional management measure relating to the use of the boat; and
  (c) the boat is on the high seas in an area covered by the regional organisation or arrangement that established the measure, and the person is reckless as to that fact.

105. Article 20(6) of the Fish Stocks Agreement.

106. Article 21(17) reads: "Where there are reasonable grounds for suspecting that a fishing vessel on the high seas is without nationality, a State may board and inspect the vessel. Where evidence so warrants, the State may take such action as may be appropriate in accordance with international law."

107. Section 88A, giving effect to Article 21.12 of the Fish Stocks Agreement.

108. There is an official note to this section, which reads as follows:

Note: Even if subsection (1) does not apply because the person holds, or acts for the holder of, a fishing concession or scientific permit, the person will commit an offence under section 95 if the person contravenes a condition of the concession or permit.

109. For further discussion of this issue, see Freestone, David. 1998. *Burden of Proof in Natural Resources Legislation: Some Critical Issues for Fisheries Law.* FAO Legislative Study 63, FAO, Rome.

110. For a report of the Technical Consultation on Illegal Unreported and Unregulated Fishing held at FAO, Rome, 2–6 October 2000, see FAO Fisheries Report No. 634.

111. Note the final preambular paragraph to the 1982 UN Convention: "Affirming that matters not regulated by this Convention continue to be governed by rules and principles of international law. . . ."

112. Article 92, 1982 UN Convention.

113. Jurisdiction based on nationality has been discussed in the context of the Convention on the Conservation of Antarctic Marine Living Resources (CCAMLR). Furthermore, the Australian Antarctic Marine Living Resources Conservation Act of 1981 applies to the activities of any Australian national or Australian vessel anywhere in the CCAMLR area. For a discussion of Norwegian practice, see T. Loebach, "Measures to be Adopted by the Port State in Combating IUU Fishing," AUS:IUU/2000/15. <http://www.affa.gov.au/ecoiuuf/papers.html>.

114. Section 113F.

115. Section 113ZE. See above for a similar provision in the Australian legislation.

116. For a discussion of the term "nationals" in the context of the high seas provisions of the 1982 UN Convention, see William Edeson, "Tools to Address IUU Fishing: The Current Legal Situation," at paragraph 34. AUS:IUU/2000/8. <http://www.affa.gov.au/ecoinf/papers.html>.

117. For a discussion of the topic in general, see Anderson, David. 1999. "Port States and Environmental Protection," in Boyle and Freestone, cited previously in note 59. See also T. Loebach, "Measures to Be Adopted by the Port State in Combating IUU Fishing." AUS:IUU/2000/15, <http://www.affa.gov.au/ecoiuuf/papers.html>; and William Edeson, "Tools to Address IUU Fishing: The Current Legal Situation." AUS:IUU/2000/8. <http://www.affa.gov.au/ecoiuuf/papers.html>.

118. Article 23.1. The article also provides in the same paragraph that the port state is not to discriminate in form or in fact against the vessels of any state, though such a condition is not present in the Compliance Agreement. Its absence may not be all that significant given that if there were such discrimination, it is possible that certain measures under the WTO Agreement would come into operation.

119. Article 23.2 of the Fish Stocks Agreement.

120. Article 23.3–Article 23.4 of the Fish Stocks Agreement states that nothing in this article affects the exercise by states of their sovereignty over ports in their territory in accordance with international law.

121. This provision gives effect to the requirement found in both agreements—namely, that a vessel must enter "voluntarily" in order for the provisions of the agreement to apply.

122. Section 4 of Regulations Relating to a Prohibition on Landing Fish Caught in Waters Outside Norwegian Jurisdiction.

123. Loebach, above note 117. Section 3 of Regulations Relating to a Prohibition on Landing Fish Caught in Waters Outside Norwegian Jurisdiction.

124. Regulations relating to fishing and hunting operations by foreign nationals in the economic zone of Norway, Royal Decree of 13 May 1977.

125. Solomon Islands Fisheries Management 1998 Act, section 56, and Nauru Fisheries Act 1997, section 26, are recent examples of how the Lacey Act provision is drafted. See, generally, Blaise Kuemlangan, "National Legislative Options to Combat IUU Fishing." AUS:IUU/2000/9. <http://www.affa.gov.au/ecoiuuf/papers.html>. This scheme is discussed in detail on p. 13.

126. See further "Legal Aspects of the Collection of Fisheries Data" by W. R. Edeson, FAO Fisheries Circular No. 953.

127. See in particular Articles 61, 62, and 119(1) of the 1982 UN Convention.

128. A problem arises in the case of certain charter and joint venture arrangements, and the Coordinating Working Party on Fishery Statistics (CWP) has formulated a test to deal with this. Basically, it has strengthened the responsibility of the flag state, exempting it from the data reporting requirements only when the vessel in question has for all practical purposes become part of the local fishing fleet of the host country, or is operating in the waters under the jurisdiction of another state, and its operation for all practical purposes is, or is intended to be, an integral part of the local economy. See further Edeson, op. cit. 1999, pp. 14–15.

www.ingramcontent.com/pod-product-compliance
Lightning Source LLC
Chambersburg PA
CBHW031811190326
41518CB00006B/285